Rainbow Savior

Rev. William A. Monday

Copyright © 2014 William Monday.

All rights reserved. No part of this book may be used or reproduced by any means, graphic, electronic, or mechanical, including photocopying, recording, taping or by any information storage retrieval system without the written permission of the publisher except in the case of brief quotations embodied in critical articles and reviews.

Scripture quotations are from The Holy Bible, English Standard Version® (ESV®), copyright © 2001 by Crossway, a publishing ministry of Good News Publishers. Used by permission. All rights reserved.

WestBow Press books may be ordered through booksellers or by contacting:

WestBow Press
A Division of Thomas Nelson & Zondervan
1663 Liberty Drive
Bloomington, IN 47403
www.westbowpress.com
1 (866) 928-1240

Because of the dynamic nature of the Internet, any web addresses or links contained in this book may have changed since publication and may no longer be valid. The views expressed in this work are solely those of the author and do not necessarily reflect the views of the publisher, and the publisher hereby disclaims any responsibility for them.

Any people depicted in stock imagery provided by Thinkstock are models, and such images are being used for illustrative purposes only. Certain stock imagery © Thinkstock.

ISBN: 978-1-4908-4555-5 (sc)
ISBN: 978-1-4908-4557-9 (hc)
ISBN: 978-1-4908-4556-2 (e)

Library of Congress Control Number: 2014913079

Printed in the United States of America.

WestBow Press rev. date: 8/20/2014

Contents

Preface ix

PART I A SHEPHERD SEEKS HIS STRAYING SHEEP 1

    1 Temple of God 3
    2 God Loves Gays 7
    3 Coming Out 13
    4 Born That Way 25
    5 Embracing True Identity 39
    6 The Diversity of Love 51
    7 The Happy Lifestyle 65
    8 No Greater Friend 71

**PART II A SHEPHERD REACHES OUT
TO HIS FLOCK** 79

    9 Welcome to Oz 81
   10 The Church for LGBTs 105
   11 Sweet Land of Liberty 121
   12 Marriage Redefined 139
   13 Somewhere over the Rainbow 161

Appendix 1: Barefoot in the Wilderness 181
Appendix 2: Barefoot in the Fold 187

This book is dedicated to a precious soul.
You are loved. No one loves you more than your Savior!

A special thanks to all the people of God who reviewed this work and offered godly encouragement and counsel for its improvement. Without the Lord's guidance through you, this work would have never been possible. May the Lord ever bless this labor of love and bring forth an eternal harvest of souls through the shed blood of Jesus Christ, the world's only Hope.

Preface

In *Rainbow Savior*, I, a pastor, am speaking to a straying sheep (Part I) and to a flock of believers (Part II) about a host of issues pertaining to homosexuality. I present a potential model for fellow Christians to follow when reaching out to others in the faith who are wrestling with this topic—especially those souls who were raised in the faith but who are presently abandoning Christ because of perceived hostility regarding their homosexuality. This work seeks to dispel that perception, while lovingly disarming—on the basis of the Holy Scriptures alone—many of the arguments in favor of homosexuality.

Seeing that so many issues involved in this discussion deal with a large number of scriptural doctrines, I have also sought to provide a refresher course on basic Christian doctrine for the edification of the Christian.

Part I

A Shepherd Seeks His Straying Sheep

1

Temple of God

You recently asked me what I thought about you now that you have come out about being gay. I could see in your eyes that you were fearful that I would see you differently, as if somehow, suddenly, you would become a stranger to me. I could see that you believed I no longer saw you as precious in my sight or in the sight of the Lord.

Truly, you don't know me as well as I thought you did. It seems that you have also lost the picture of how the Lord sees you, which enables you to look at yourself with all confidence and without shame. My words to you are your chance to truly know me and my love for you in Christ as a pastor to his precious lamb. This work before you is also your chance to remember what the Lord has made you to be in him. The Lord's own Word is the path for you to see infinite worth in yourself again.

If only you could know how many times I have remembered you in my prayers before the Father! If only you could know how much your mom and dad and other Christians who know you have prayed for you before the throne of God! We only want the Lord to bless you in every way.

Let me begin by sharing with you how I see you, and why every word written here was penned for *you*. Do you know what your Lord said about you in the Holy Scriptures the moment you were brought to faith in him? The apostle Paul put it this way: "Do you not know that you are God's temple and that God's Spirit dwells in you?" (1 Corinthians 3:16). A little later, he echoed the same sentiment with an added word of encouragement: "Do you not know that your body is a temple of the Holy Spirit within you, whom you have from God? You are not your own, for you were bought with a price. So glorify God in your body" (1 Corinthians 6:19–20). Using the brush of the Holy Scriptures, I paint my picture of you. The temple referred to in 1 Corinthians 3 and 6—which now includes every Christian—is you, and I still believe, deep down, that you are fighting the good fight to remain in Christ. Keep fighting!

The word used for "temple" in 1 Corinthians is special. Arguably, there's nothing more special than this word. In this section of Scripture, the word *temple* is the same word used for the greatest temple ever constructed on earth, Solomon's temple, which was built to be a true representation of God's holy sanctuary in heaven, the place where God dwells in all his glory (Hebrews 9:24).

The word especially denotes the innermost place of Solomon's temple. The innermost place is known as the Holy of Holies where, in the Old Testament, only the high priest could enter once a year. In those days, people believed that God would manifest his presence to the high priest in order to bless him, all of God's people, and the rest of the world.

Dear child of God, that's who you are! In Christ, you are the magnificent temple where God has chosen to dwell! How, then, could I not care for you or count you among God's people? In all truth, how are you not a part of the most precious family in all the earth? At the same time, you need to know how the body of believers' concern for you has grown because of your choices and this LGBT[1] advocacy.

In the centuries after Solomon built God's temple as his dwelling, God's people abandoned him. In the face of their endless rebellion,

---

[1] Lesbian, Gay, Bisexual, Transgender. Sometimes a *Q* is affixed to the end of this acronym, which stands for *queer*. This is an acronym the gay community has adopted for itself.

God allowed calamity to befall his magnificent temple. Out of love—tough love—God allowed the Babylonians to come and destroy the place of his presence among his people. The result was that God's people became a deserted people. God was no longer with them.

In those days, there was a prophet named Jeremiah. He was called the weeping prophet, and it was for this simple reason: he was there to see God's people wither away in unbelief and immorality. He was there to see the temple burn, which happened simply because so very few would listen to God's Word anymore. Finally, according to tradition, Jeremiah himself was taken off to Egypt, because the temple was gone and all the land was in ruin. The people were scattered and lost. And in Egypt, according to tradition, Jeremiah was stoned to death, although he was faithful to God's Word. He was stoned to death by God's enemies for his faithfulness to God and the truth. There's no wondering why he was called the weeping prophet.

Dear temple of God, don't let the people of this world trample over you. Don't let this issue overtake you and plant the seeds of unbelief and immorality in your heart to destroy you like the temple of old. Don't let me become a weeping prophet over you, a precious lamb for whom the Great Shepherd bled and died!

Sit with me a little while now. Read over these words written down for you and for all who can relate to what you are going through. Would you be willing to reason together in the Lord? You don't need to be afraid of me, and I pray that you won't grow hostile toward me either. We are allies in all of this.

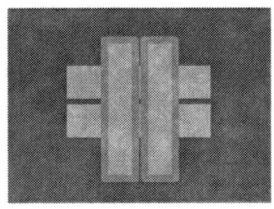

2

God Loves Gays

Equal in Love

"God loves gays. *'For God so loved the world*, that he gave his only Son, that whoever believes in him should not perish but have eternal life' (John 3:16). Aren't gay people a part of the world God loves? And if God loves gay people, then God loves me, so what's the problem? I'm saved. I trust in Jesus. Why won't my pastor just let me be?" So goes your reasoning and the reasoning of so many others.

Precious temple of God, there is more to this verse than the way it's being used these days. To be sure, I have no doubt that God loves you. I know he does. To be sure, "God so loved" everybody—gays and all—when Jesus poured out his blood for everyone on the cross (Romans 5:8). At the same time, there's the other side of this truth, which is almost entirely overlooked today, and it's a truth that I'm praying you'll be willing to let me share with you in love.

Equal in Desperation

If everyone is loved by God equally, we need to realize this: God loves us, but not for what we are in our sinful condition or for what we do in our fallen state. He loves us *in spite of* these things. The Bible goes on to point out this sobering truth about our desperation when it declares in another place, "All have turned aside; *together they have become worthless*; *no one does good, not even one*" (Romans 3:12, emphasis added). This passage is telling us that we are all in a desperate state when God loves us, and that it is a miracle for him to love any one of us at any time! The fact, then, that we enjoy a reality where God loves us for Christ's sake is nothing short of a miracle.

The truth about our equal desperation to be loved runs throughout the Scriptures and is even referred to in the latter part of John 3:16. Toward the end of that verse, Jesus goes on to say that "whoever believes in him *should not perish* but have eternal life." What is the reason for this point about "perishing," unless it is true that we all are equally desperate for God's love, that we are *not okay*, not saved, as we are?

Precious child of God, good people, righteous people—*loveable* people—don't perish. Only wicked people perish, and the sobering reality from the latter half of John 3:16 is that we are all equally wicked and condemned in our natural state for what we do apart from God's love. *Part of trusting in Jesus and being saved, then, means calling out to him to save us from who we are and what we are doing before we perish. It means turning our back on all that makes us worthless.*

Jesus proclaimed both the amazing truth of God's love and the sobering truth of our desperation for it in John 3:16 in yet another way: through his sacrificial work on the cross. In other words, God gave up his only Son for a reason. It was not for righteous people that Jesus came and died, but for the desperate ones whom the Bible labels as "sinners" (Mark 2:17). As I shared before, those who are righteous don't need a savior (Galatians 2:21). However, since there is no one righteous on his own in God's sight (Romans 3:20), God gave his Son to die for all the world, for all whose condition and actions he hates equally, whether we are speaking about the best person you can think of or the worst. "God shows his love for us in that *while we were still sinners, Christ died for us*" (Romans 5:8).

Here's my point about God's love: God gave his love to us in Christ, not so that we would remain as we are, but so that we would turn away from ourselves and all that we are doing against God. This truth applies to all people, of course, including me.

I, your pastor, am not worthy of God's love, either by my nature or my actions. I am no more worthy of God's love than anybody else. I am no more worthy of his love than Hitler, to put it bluntly, and how that truth cuts to the heart! I too need to call out to Jesus to save me from what I am and what I do by nature. Having proven this through the Scriptures, especially in John 3:16, we need to move on to discuss what, in particular, we need to turn away from so that we never perish. This demands some judging on our part, judging of who we are and of whatever we are doing against the Lord's will.

Equal in Judging

Jesus' teachings about the humble attitude required for judging ought to remain at the forefront of our minds, especially as some of the words of this book become difficult for both of us.

> Judge not, and you will not be judged; condemn not, and you will not be condemned ... Why do you see the speck that is in your brother's eye, but do not notice the log that is in your own eye? How can you say to your brother, "Brother, let me take out the speck that is in your eye," when you yourself do not see the log that is in your own eye? You hypocrite, *first take the log out of your own eye, and then you will see clearly to take out the speck that is in your brother's eye.* (Luke 6:37–38, 41–42, emphasis added)

Notice that Jesus is not saying, "Don't ever point out something that's wrong with someone else." If that were the case, he never would have concluded by saying, "Then you will see clearly to take out the speck in your brother's eye." Those of us who quote Jesus, saying "Judge not lest ye be judged" and believe that we should never point out anything wrong in someone else have missed out on Jesus' true teaching. Jesus *does* want us to judge what is right and what is wrong. He wants us to judge, however, not by coming up with our own condemning standard but by declaring from God's Word what he has judged as right and wrong already. Jesus pointed us to a godly kind of judging when he said, "Make a right judgment!" (John 7:24).

There will be specks in your eyes. There surely have been logs and specks in mine. Love compels us to help each other when we're in danger or when we're hurting because of sin, even when the one who's in danger or hurting can't see past blinding logs and specks. It would be unloving for me not to help you and point things out to you when you are in need. The same goes for me. Love does not refrain from speaking the truth but "rejoices with the truth" (1 Corinthians 13:6b).

Can you see how this teaching of the Scripture about judging in humility engenders compassion for all others, even as it teaches that no one is better or worse than another, that they are equal? Can you see how this promotes understanding? Without these Scriptures to point out our equality in every way, we all become prejudiced in some way. We will either support gays and hate bigots, or we will become bigots and hate gays. Neither of these approaches is what the Lord desires.

Equal Through and Through

As we move ahead in this discussion, we must move forward as equals. Are you and I willing to admit that we are equally loved by God, even though we are on opposite sides of the LGBT issue? Are you and I willing to admit that we are all equally desperate for the love that God offers to each of us, no matter what side we are on? Once true equality is established between you and me—something we all desire—the next step for us is to discuss what the specific speck might be in your eye or mine. We must begin the process of judging humbly and by God's righteous standard alone. To ensure equality, we will point out all the logs in my eyes and in the eyes of Christians like me. It's only fair. It's what our Lord calls for. It's the way of true love.

At this point in our talk, dear temple of God, I only ask that you'd be willing to agree with me that no one is perfect, and that includes your pastor. I don't suppose that would be too difficult a thing to do. How often does a pastor give someone an invitation to call him a sinner, or even the chief of sinners (1 Timothy 1:15)? Can you also be so perceptive as to agree that we are all sinners, including you? Finally, can you agree that we are all in need of being made sinless in order to be with our holy God? If so, then you can surely see me as your friend, one who would even give up his life for you (John 15:13)—and I would. I truly only want what's best for you.

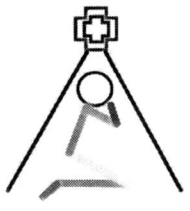

3

Coming Out

Into the Light

I can still remember when a loved one of yours broke the news to me that you had come out. In a way—and this may come as a surprise to you—I'm glad you came out. Did you know that I'm actually all for people and their coming out with whatever they need to share? I'm absolutely serious about that. Why should anyone ever feel like they have to hide something—or, worse yet, hide themselves? What kind of life would that be? How hard your life must have been up to that point, although I realize it probably isn't much easier now. You should know that I believe everybody should come out about anything as much as they need to. I'd even encourage a coming-out at least once a week. In fact, isn't this the historic practice of the church?

Every Sunday in the safe community of the church, I boldly come out with all that I am and all the evil I have done. You've been doing the same from early on, whether you recognize it or not. I know that this is not the same as what it means for LGBTs to come out. My point for now is to simply encourage you and me and everyone else to lay all our cards out on the table, no matter what they are. That is an admirable practice. Many might not realize that this is an ancient practice in the historic Christian church. In a very real sense,

Christians have been coming out for thousands of years, and you are a part of that heritage.

As to the Christian brand of coming-out in the church's practice of confession and absolution, I admit that I am a sinner. In this confession, I also admit that I deserve absolute punishment in this life and in the afterlife for the evil I've done and the good I've left undone, whether in thought, word, or action. Does this sound familiar to you? Of course it does. You know these words by heart, and you should know that when I confess my sins publicly every Sunday, I do so with all sincerity. It hasn't always been easy to be this open and honest, but I've learned not to be ashamed of doing it—and it does take some learning. It's not that I don't regret my sin or that I have become so calloused to it that it's easy to confess. It's just that I have learned that hiding it away is never the answer. The answer is to do the exact opposite and come clean.

What helped me to come out about my sin was to realize that God knows everything anyway. He's convinced me that it's best to tell him *before* he calls me to give an account. More importantly, he has provided the most comforting solution in the way of complete, free, and full forgiveness for all my faults through the blood of Christ (Hebrews 10:10–12). I know that you know this, but please indulge me a little more here. We can so easily forget how God's grace works.

In the Scriptures, God further encourages me to come out about my sins. He reminds me that he especially hopes to find broken and contrite hearts in order to heal them (Psalm 51:17). He even tells me that he and all the angels rejoice over anyone who repents of his sin (Luke 15:7). This, in fact, was one of the reasons Jesus came into the world. About the general concept of coming out—if we can be so bold as to use that terminology in this context—Jesus said, "I have come into this world as light, so that whoever believes in me may not remain in darkness" (John 12:46). Wouldn't that be something if the whole world could be a safe place for those who desperately need to come out about anything? Whether something is good or bad, coming out ought to be encouraged by all. That's the only point I'm driving at here. So, in a very real sense, I'm glad you have come out about following the gay lifestyle.

Now, let's address the kind of coming-out that gay people are often encouraged to do, the kind of coming-out you experienced. There are those who think that coming out about homosexuality is something to be praised, not something to repent over or receive absolution for. In my opinion, an ever-increasing number of people think about coming out as if it's akin to an awards banquet, complete with rolling out the red carpet.[2] Today, LGBTs who come out about their lifestyle are honored in public in much the same way as a teen who makes the honor roll at school or honorable mention on the athletic field.

The challenge of this section is for us to figure out how to come out about homosexuality. Should it really be like walking down the red carpet, or does it fall under the umbrella of confessing sin and receiving forgiveness like all other sin? I know that people on both sides of the issue may already have made up their minds on this, but can one side or the other be certain they've come to the right conclusion? Some say it's not a sin. Others say it is. You seem to be somewhere in the middle, although you are clearly leaning to the side of the LGBT community. Surely both sides can't be right. Neither is it beneficial to be stuck in the middle. So, who decides the issue?

Whatever the case, I want to assure you that I do believe that homosexuality needs to be brought out into the light, and that there ought to be a safe place for this to happen. I want you to know that there is a safe place with me, and with Christians like me, where you can confess anything. Remember that we are all equals and equal in our struggles. Those for or against homosexuality ought to at least agree to let it come out, in hopes that all may learn how to deal with it appropriately.

---

[2] Among many examples, I recall President Obama's address in a press conference where he praised Jason Collins, an NBA star, for coming out about being gay (April 30, 2013). http://www.huffingtonpost.com/2013/04/30/obama-jason-collins-press-conference_n_3185134.html

Rev. William A. Monday

Discerning between Good and Evil

How do you know what is good and what is evil? It's a question that prompts a couple more: Is there such a thing as good? Is there such a thing as evil? People have all sorts of opinions on this. Yet most people would agree that it is essential for society to keep some bearings about which ways are evil and which ways are good. The proof is in the fact that, from day to day, many of us naturally make numerous distinctions in our minds concerning good and evil. These decisions we make are what provide order to our society.

For example, would anyone have a problem in condemning Hitler's actions or the actions of pedophiles? We all know that their deeds are pure evil. We know it is okay to make that judgment. Regarding them, no one ever seems to quote Jesus' words, "Judge not, lest ye be judged." We also know that if a majority of us approved of what Hitler did or what pedophiles do, our society would crumble. This world would be a literal hell. Surely the vast majority, if not everybody, would agree with this idea. To argue that there's no such thing as right and wrong, or that there's no real way of knowing which is which, is, at best, impractical. At worst, it is our downfall.

But for argument's sake, how do you and I know for certain that Hitler and pedophiles are guilty of doing unspeakable things? Is it God who decides that? If not, then who? Do you? Do I? How about a majority? If the majority decides, wouldn't that inevitably lead to the oppression of those in the minority? And if a minority decides, isn't that unfair to the majority?

I believe that God gave us his Law, among other things, that we might distinguish right from wrong clearly, and I believe this is the only way to rightly divide good from evil. This is something you also were raised to believe. I believe that God's Law alone, along with all of his Word, is the sole authority that people are to use to discern good and evil absolutely. This is what the Holy Bible teaches, and this is why passages from the Bible are found throughout my words to you. There is no other authority to which we can look. There is no other power that can truly change our minds.³ That being the case, may I have a moment to dust off some of your studies in the Word from years past?

The Scriptures say that God wrote his divine Law first in our hearts, and then he went on to give each of us a conscience as a judge. The conscience is what makes us feel good when we do right by the Law and rotten when we break it (Romans 2:14–15). It is an invaluable gift, and we would do well to listen to it. However, the Scriptures also say that this knowledge in our hearts—including the voice of our conscience—is not entirely reliable because of our sinful corruption.⁴

As to our consciences, we often sear them as we grow callous to what is evil (1 Timothy 4:2). We can end up killing our consciences, if we aren't careful. Furthermore, the Scriptures say that evil has so corrupted us that there's nothing sicker than our own hearts. The human heart is beyond all cure. Who can begin to understand the error of his ways, or who can understand the human heart, which leads us all in so many wrong directions? (Jeremiah 17:9). Since this is the case, we may want to reconsider the popular counsel of our day: "Follow your heart!" Everyone seems to be offering this counsel as advice to anyone uncertain about anything.

Beware! It's because of this manmade philosophy about right and wrong and the fickle nature of our hearts that the proverb reads, "Many ways seem right to a man but in the end they lead to death" (Proverbs 16:25). That's a proverb that speaks not only to our depraved hearts but to our flawed human reasoning and our depraved intellect. All our thinking is corrupted by sin. Add to this another biblical idea

---

³ Although apologetics—the use of sanctified human reason to combat sinful human reason to make a way to embrace the Scriptures—can be useful on LGBT issues, I have intentionally abandoned that pursuit to simply let the Word do its work. This is due to my understanding of who you are and the background you have in the Scriptures. Ultimately, the Word alone has the answers.

⁴ In sharing this truth concerning our sinful corruption, I do not wish to devalue the gift of conscience. The conscience should always be followed—until the gift of God's Word, the only certain authority, can prove a conscience right or wrong.

that all our intents are evil from childhood (Genesis 8:21), and it's obvious that we still need some help in distinguishing good from evil. Actually, we need a lot of help, not just on the finer points of good and evil either, but on the major points too.

God, therefore, gave his divine Law to Moses on Mt. Sinai in divine revelation. God gave his Law to make the distinction between good and evil absolutely clear for us so that we would never have to wonder. John 1:17 says that the Law came through Moses. Romans 5:20 echoes the same truth, as it adds that the purpose of this revealed Law is to spell out all evil completely. God's purpose in showing us the true nature of our sin by his Law is to prove that no one will be made acceptable to God by attempting to keep his Law (Romans 3:20). It's plain to see from the Scriptures that the Word of God is the only trustworthy authority to distinguish between good and evil.

At this point, we need only to acknowledge that most people object to the use of the Scriptures, which includes God's Law, as the absolute authority to decide right from wrong. If you are inclined to question whether the Bible is the sole authority on right or wrong, I want you to know that I understand. There are those who reason that, at best, the Bible is just one authority to help us decide. Still others suggest that the Bible is full of errors and that there are some laws there which no one follows, nor should they. If I'm not mistaken, most in the LGBT community, if not all, and many who support homosexuality, hold to one or the other of these opinions—if they haven't written off the Bible altogether.

If you deny the authority of the Scripture to decide the LGBT issue at hand, I would encourage you to consider other questions for yourself: What authority *would* you appeal to in order to distinguish good from evil? Who or what defines it? If not divine revelation, then what else could be as reliable? Do you think people would be foolish to consider the Bible the sole authority on good and evil? If all humans are indeed sinful, as the Bible proclaims, then it goes without saying that we are incapable by our nature to distinguish between good and evil, at least absolutely.

My guess is that these questions are probably something new to you, but I would encourage you to think through them. Though the answers may be many and varied in your mind, I want you to know that this present line of questioning will all boil down to one of two things: it's either to-each-his-own when distinguishing between good and evil, or it's God alone who must differentiate between the one and the other through his Holy Word. There is really no other way to decide anything on matters of good and evil. We can't have it both ways. Trying to play both sides will only lead to a contradictory and conflicted life.

Whatever you think right now about biblical authority, you should know that whoever denies God's Word as the absolute authority stands in disagreement with Jesus Christ and the apostle Paul, along with all the prophets and apostles. Furthermore, if someone believes that those who hold to the Bible alone as their authority are foolish—inadvertently, I presume—such a one would be calling Jesus and his apostles and prophets fools too. Isn't that what Pontius Pilate[5] thought about Jesus before he had him crucified? To Jesus' claim that he alone had a monopoly on truth, Pilate mockingly asked, "What is truth?", as if no one could possibly know. That is to say that Pontius Pilate refused to accept God's answer to the question that this chapter seeks to address: what is the sole authority to decide right from wrong? My fear is that Pilate isn't alone these days in his opinion that we really can't be sure about truth or knowing right from wrong.

Pilate's denial of absolutes was in response to Jesus' bold claim that he was born for the sole purpose of testifying to the truth and that all who are on the side of truth listen to him (John 18:37–38). How Jesus' claim before Pilate supports biblical authority is found earlier in John's gospel. In John 5:39–40, Jesus claimed that the Scriptures all pointed to him: "It is [the Scriptures] that bear witness about

---

[5] Pontius Pilate was the Roman governor over the land of the Jews, which included the area where Jesus ministered. Pilate was responsible for handing Jesus over to be crucified. Pilate asked Jesus the question about truth when Jesus was on trial for his life.

me." In another place, Jesus said that the Scriptures were infallible (John 10:35b). This would include the part about God's putting the Law on our hearts and giving the Law completely through Moses. In essence, Jesus claimed that all the words of the Scriptures were his words.

Be sure of this: both Jesus and Paul pointed to the Holy Bible as the sole authority on good and evil, life and truth. The apostle Paul's thoughts from 2 Timothy 3:16–17 show that he saw the Scriptures alone as sufficient for people to learn of their salvation and be guided into every good work. In Titus 2:12, he went on to say that the Word alone teaches us to say no to all evil by the power of the gospel. I am including the New Testament with the Old in my definition of the Scriptures, because Jesus commissioned his disciples to record his own words in those pages by direction of his Spirit, and Paul, under inspiration, ended up writing about half the New Testament (John 14:26; 2 Peter 3:16).

If you still confess to be a Christian, I'm asking you to do the honest thing and embrace the Scriptural view of Jesus and Paul, not a worldly view that opposes them. Many people like to think of Jesus, and perhaps Paul, as merely good teachers and moralists on some points but not on others. This is a contradiction for the Christian. Jesus and Paul can only be good if everything they said in the Scripture was true, especially because of the claims they made about the Christ and about God.

Jesus claimed to be the Christ and the Savior of all, and Paul claimed to be his apostle. Because of such claims, Jesus is either the Savior—which means that the Bible is God's truth alone—or Jesus is the greatest deceiver this world has ever known, and nothing is trustworthy in the Bible. That includes anything about morality found there. Could Jesus really be a good teacher or a moral person if he was leading the world astray from God? There's no in-between position. Jesus never gave us the option of holding on to some parts of what he said, while denying other sections. Precious temple of God, it really is all or nothing when it comes to our view of the Bible.

If the Bible is not the authority, I would ask that you help me understand what authority we should look to for the standards that need to be set for our lives. Should we look to the government? Should we look to the majority? Should we leave it up to scholars, celebrities, or philosophers? Should we leave it up to the individual? Is it up to our collective feelings, reasoning, and intellect?

If you have something better than the Bible, then, out of love for me and my soul, please let me know. Wouldn't love for God call for you to enlighten me and show me what God has really been saying—if he has not been speaking through the Holy Scriptures? The point is this: none of us is an island. People care for you, and we all know that God wants us to care for each other by speaking the truth in love (Ephesians 4:15). This is the outstanding debt we owe to each other (Romans 13:8).

Ultimately, there's no way to convince anyone to hold to biblical authority to rightfully distinguish between good and evil. I can't convince you to cling to the Scriptures alone. Trust me; I would if I could. Only the goodness of the Holy Bible can persuade us, and God alone must accomplish that. But think of this: if Adam and Eve, who were perfect, fell into temptation to doubt God's Word regarding what was good and evil (Genesis 3:1–8), what chance do we have in our corrupt state to recognize one from the other, especially if we are consciously rejecting his Word? I only ask that you recognize that holding to the Bible is a miraculous feat. Thankfully, it's a miracle that God wants to accomplish in our hearts. May we not get in the way of that!

Lastly, if you are leaning toward rejecting biblical authority, we still need to realize the seriousness of the situation in trying to approach the issue of homosexuality. Consider another practical truth in the Scriptures: "Do not be deceived. God is not mocked, for whatever one sows, that will he also reap" (Galatians 6:7). That is to say, if we strive to define what is good and what is evil apart from God—who alone is good and defines everything for us to save us from evil—we won't be able to bring any truth to light. We will simply miss out on what is good for us and will be overcome by what is detrimental to both body and soul. And in the darkness, without the light of truth, we won't even know what evil is doing to us until it's too late.

We're at a fork in the road. Precious temple of God, you must decide in faith what your authority is going to be in order to distinguish between good and evil. I'm asking a little more of you now than I did in the previous section. I'm going to keep asking for more as we go along, but I hope you can trust that I only want what's good for you. If you come up with your own authority to replace the Bible, you can stop reading this long letter of mine to you. There's no point in going on, because we will surely end up disagreeing on some of the points to be made. But before you put down this work of love for you, let's move on to one more thought.

Enlightenment

If you are willing and open minded, we can go down the narrow road of the Scriptures with the possibility that it might very well be God's authority and the only authority there is. It is hardly blind faith, if you look to the Bible. Arguably the greatest figure in human history, Jesus Christ held to this book alone as God's Word. He used the Old Testament to support his claim that he was the Christ and that he would even conquer death for us (Luke 24:44–48). Think of that before passing over the Bible or looking at it as inferior in any way. Return to your upbringing, even if by chance it feels too far off in the distance of your rearview mirror.

With Jesus raised from the dead, you have something no one else can offer you. The resurrected Lord gave testimony to this one book and its truthfulness. In other words, if a dead guy comes back from the grave and says, "Hold to this book alone! It's the Word of God!", we might do well to give it another shot and hold on to it in all that it proclaims. Could there be anything weightier than a resurrected man's testimony?

Jesus was constantly referring to the Scriptures in his ministry as if it were a playbook he was executing. He did nothing apart from those sacred words. The same was true for the apostles after the resurrection of our Lord. According to tradition, all the disciples of Jesus who were in his inner circle sealed their testimony about Jesus in their own blood. They all became martyrs for Christ and for what was written in the Scripture. As for John, the beloved, though he did not die a martyr's death, he spent many years at the end of his life in prison for his testimony. To his dying breath, he never turned his back on his faith. I remind you of this so that you can grow in your confidence about the Word and believe that it is to be our all in all!

Add to this truth the Bible's historical accuracy, its fulfilled prophecies, and its unity of theme and unique message of grace, in spite of its forty different authors over 1,500 years of writing. Consider how it satisfies the major life questions that ring true to what we experience in our human condition. Think about the manner of its preservation over the centuries and the fact that it can boast about having the greatest impact on human history. When you do, I know you'll find that we can have no more credible authority. The Bible testifies of itself, claiming to be the divinely inspired Word of God, which—surprisingly or not so surprisingly—few other books declare about themselves. Even many religious scriptures do not make divine claims about their authorship (2 Peter 1:16–18, 21). Allow me to plead with you not to give up the treasure that has been passed down to you from previous generations, even from saints who are now finished with all the struggles of this life.

Dear temple of God, no other standard—including our own minds and hearts—compares to the Bible. Arguably, there is no work other than the Bible that is as widely accepted and has stood the test of time. Compare the authority of the Bible to that of all other sources to which we often look. I would argue that there is no real comparison at all. Do you still believe the Scriptures as you were taught, or have you forgotten much of this? Wherever you are in your beliefs, it's not too late! There's still time to return to all these things written for you in the Word!

You can trust God. You can trust the Lord who created you, redeemed you, and sanctified you for a truly happy life.[6] You can trust the Bible, which not only claims but is proven to be God's Word by Jesus' resurrection from the dead. You can trust this path above all others. If you and I commit to holding such a view, it's a guaranteed certainty that we will find a road that will bless us in every way. We will truly find the one way that God has established to make us all happy and safe as he points out all good from all evil, all righteousness from every sin.

What is your authority? Is your mind open or closed about the possibility that the Bible alone will make all things clear? Whatever you decide, I hope you feel that you can "come out" about your view on the Bible. In the hopes that you will come out in favor of it once more, allow me to share with you now the kind of love found within the Scriptures, a love that is hardly known, a love that you yourself may not entirely remember, a love that will be there for you as long as you breathe.

---

[6] Biblical happiness (blessedness) is defined differently from worldly happiness. Worldly happiness revolves around selfishness and instant gratification, regardless of other important things, like people or virtues. Happiness in a biblical sense involves struggle and hardship, but it is a struggle that is more than worthwhile, because it is a struggle to do what is good in light of all the goodness God gives to us (1 Peter 2:20b–21). Moses' life comes to mind as just one example: "By faith Moses, when he was grown up, refused to be called the son of Pharaoh's daughter, choosing rather to be mistreated with the people of God than to enjoy the fleeting pleasures of sin. He considered the reproach of Christ greater wealth than the treasures of Egypt, for he was looking to the reward" (Hebrews 11:24–26). The chapter entitled "The Happy Lifestyle" will cover this concept in more detail.

4

Born That Way

Born Gay

"I am gay. I'm born that way." How those words must have pierced the hearts of all who love you so much in the Lord. But can I tell you something about the time when you spoke those words to me? I'm not at all surprised. Oh, to be sure, it was a shock at first to hear it from you, but I'm not surprised that anyone would ever say, "I'm gay. I'm born that way." (Please forgive me, by the way, if you sensed that I was shocked and could not believe my ears. It doesn't mean I don't care for you. The Lord knows I do care, and with all the love of Christ. Who sits down to write a book for someone else if they don't care?)

Do you want to know why I'm not surprised that someone would say, "I am gay. I'm born that way."? It's because, in a very real sense, the Bible supports the claim. The Bible said long ago that we are all indeed born a certain way, a way that you are branding with the label of "being gay." There are many other labels for how we are born, ways that people gravitate toward. The label of being born gay shouldn't be understood as any different from one of those other labels.

Let me explain what I'm saying. According to Psalm 51:5, we are all born sinful. King David wrote, "Behold, I was brought forth in iniquity, and in sin did my mother conceive me." The reference here is not to any act of David's mother. The passage is speaking to the nature of how we are all born into this world. We are all born sinful.

Ultimately, Psalm 51:5—along with other verses, such as James 2:10 and Romans 7:8a—teaches that we were all born with the capacity to become any kind of sinner there is. You, therefore, were born with the capacity to be gay, as was everybody. It's possible that you were even born predisposed to that particular type of sin, perhaps more than others. You—in what you are claiming—are simply embracing your natural birth in a very specific way.

If you want more proof about how you were born, let me share with you a thought from the apostle Paul's words in Romans 7. The apostle said, "Sin, seizing an opportunity through the commandment, produced in me all kinds of covetousness" (Romans 7:8). That is to say, sin produces in all our hearts a desire for everything forbidden. To *covet* means to desire something God forbids. Since God forbids all forms of sexual immorality in the sixth commandment—"You shall not commit adultery" (Exodus 20:14)—Paul was telling us that we naturally desire all forms of sexual immorality.[7] This includes all forms of homosexuality, because homosexuality is a sin. Some may prefer homosexuality over other kinds of sin, while others may prefer other forms of immorality over homosexuality. In our sinfulness, we can even seemingly be repulsed by one sin in preference of another.

---

[7] The sixth commandment on adultery includes both the married and unmarried alike and all sexual immorality. Jesus' teaching in Matthew 5 makes that perfectly clear. In his Sermon on the Mount, Jesus declared, "You have heard that it was said, 'Do not commit adultery!' But I say to you that everyone who looks at a woman with lustful intent has already committed adultery" (Matthew 5:28). Here Jesus said that adultery is any form of sexuality outside of marriage. In this verse, Jesus goes so far as to say that longing for—just thinking about—anything sexual outside of marriage with another person is breaking God's commandment. Who of us isn't guilty of breaking this commandment in some way, whether gay or straight?

Whether we struggle to believe that idea or not, this is what the Bible declares.[8]

Should anyone who knows the Scriptures be surprised if someone says, "I'm gay. I'm born that way."? No. Indeed, the Bible supports your claim in a very real sense. At the same time, it would be a fallacy for anyone to believe that because one is born a certain way, God must have made them that way and that it's okay. One would also be in error to think that a person can't be changed in regard to how they were born. God can do all things (Matthew 19:26).

By my opening words in this chapter, it has become absolutely clear that I am indeed calling homosexuality a sin. The Scriptures declare this condition and lifestyle—among many others—to be in conflict with God's will. The reason, then, for beginning this chapter by stating the truth that we all have the capacity to be gay is in the hope of pointing out sin apart from any condemnatory tone.

Precious temple of God, remember that we are all born the same. We are all born as sinners. You have your sins, and I have mine, but no one is better or worse than another. The issue now becomes one of whether or not we want to remain in our sin or leave it behind as Jesus urged the woman to do in John 8:1–11. The woman was guilty of a form of sexual immorality—just like you, just like me, just like everybody.

The following is what the Scriptures have to say to those who practice homosexuality *willfully*. My question to you is this: are you *willfully practicing homosexuality*, or are you struggling against it? Whatever the case, the Scriptures can only help and make all things clear for you, wherever you are.

---

[8] The issue of being "born that way" speaks to the doctrine of original sin and our human depravity, which, contrary to the opinion of many, is total.

Rev. William A. Monday

Spiritually Stillborn

The Holy Scriptures declare that we were born dead in our transgressions (Ephesians 2:1–3). The symptoms that prove we came into this world spiritually stillborn are found in the dead existence of our sinful acts, which we all "live" in. Actually, in the Greek language of the New Testament, the phrase *to live in sin* means literally "to walk about in sin" (Ephesians 2:2). In other words, to "live in sin" is a zombie existence. The Bible refuses to acknowledge living in willful sin as any kind of living at all.

The homosexual condition and lifestyle—among a multitude of other patterns of "living"—is counted among the ways of a dead existence. The point about homosexuality being a "lifestyle" among other sinful patterns can't be emphasized enough. Homosexuality is listed among a host of other sins that infect all of us equally, and just as equally, God delivers all of us from those sins through Jesus Christ. Christians need to treat homosexuality like any other sin and love the sinner—just as we sinners, generally speaking, are all unconditionally loved by God.

In 1 Corinthians 6:9–10, Paul wrote about homosexuality. He was writing to Christians who were in danger of being entangled in that sin, among so many other things. I pray that you are encouraged to see that you are not the only Christian who has dealt with this sin or the temptation toward it. You are not alone!

Paul said, "Do you not know that the unrighteous will not inherit the Kingdom of God? Do not be deceived: neither the sexually immoral, nor idolaters, nor adulterers, nor men who practice homosexuality, nor thieves, nor the greedy, nor drunkards, nor revilers, nor swindlers will inherit the Kingdom of God." Here we note very clearly that homosexuality is a sin.[9] More importantly, we

---

[9] Some argue that Paul was not specifically pointing out homosexuality as a sin but rather the *abuses* of homosexuality that were found in his society, such as pederasty or ritual prostitution. Such ones suggest that the issue is not one of sexuality but of abuse, control, and domination over others. Others argue that a passage

see that a willful practice of it excludes a person from entering into the sinless kingdom of God. How so?

Faith in the Savior—the prerequisite for entering into the kingdom of God (Matthew 22:12)—cannot exist where sin is knowingly embraced and accepted (1 John 1:7–9). We can't cling by faith to the one who saves us from sin, if we're refusing to let go of our sin. To put it another way, no one may enter into the perfect kingdom of God while embracing his sin. So many Christians are confused on this point in distinguishing willful sin from sins of weakness. Neither type of sin is desirable. While sins of weakness can become willful sin, willful sin can only put us in immediate danger of losing our salvation. It's imperative that we recognize the difference.

Again, homosexuality isn't the only sinful condition or lifestyle. Paul also included in his list any sexual conduct apart from marriage, whether gay or straight (internet pornography, a date that goes too far, a one-night stand, cohabitation, adultery, and so on). It's not just sexual sin either. Paul called out the greedy and drunkards too, among many others.

Paul didn't list these sins to shame anyone. Besides, we're all guilty of these things, and that includes the apostle Paul. He was only speaking to those who willfully practice these sins, in order that they might not lose out on eternal life. He wanted to show that Christ saved us all from those things by giving Christians a change of heart. Paul's hope was that his people would stop embracing those sins which would otherwise condemn them.

Right after Paul spoke against the willful practice of any sin, he shared his hope for his people: "And such were some of you. But you

---

like this speaks generally, through specific details, of loveless acts, which don't include all forms of homosexuality. Still others say that passages like this were for Paul's time and culture and no longer apply to us today. The same arguments are used against Paul's parallel address of homosexuality in Romans 1:20–2:1 and 1 Timothy 1:9-11. However, the general term for "sexual immorality" includes all forms of homosexuality. It also includes all forms of heterosexuality outside of marriage. This definition for sexual immorality becomes evident with Jesus' own words on sexuality in Matthew 19:1–12, which we will come to in a moment.

were washed, you were sanctified, you were justified in the name of the Lord Jesus Christ and by the Spirit of our God." Like Jesus, Paul spoke with no condemning tone against people who struggle in their sin or are trapped in it.[10]

Speaking of Jesus, there's a popular idea out there that he never spoke about homosexuality and, therefore, never spoke against it.[11] Some suggest that only the apostle Paul spoke against that condition in his letters—as if Paul came up with new doctrines apart from Jesus. If that were the case, Jesus would not have commissioned Paul as one sent from him, nor would Christ's church have recognized Paul as an apostle, especially considering his pre-conversion agenda to round up Christians and see them killed (Acts 9:1–19). It is unfair to pit Jesus against Paul or to declare Paul's writings, in this regard, as irrelevant for today.

Whoever would say that Jesus didn't address homosexuality or see it as sin is in error of the Scripture. Jesus addressed all sexuality on one occasion when people brought up the topic of marriage to him. We read about this account in Matthew 19:1–12.

> Now when Jesus had finished these sayings, he went away from Galilee and entered the region of Judea beyond the Jordan. And large crowds followed him, and he healed them there.
>
> And Pharisees came up to him and tested him by asking, "Is it lawful to divorce one's wife for any cause?" He answered, "Have you not read that he who created

---

[10] As to any time in the Scripture where there is a condemnatory tone toward people—and there are those places (Isaiah 1–5; Galatians 1; Matthew 23; Luke 10; etc.)—words of condemnation are directed toward those who refuse to listen to God's Word and have hardened themselves in their sin and falsehood to the point that they boldly encourage others to do the same. We should not be mistaken and think that the Lord does not condemn people who refuse his Word and who lead others into the same sins.

[11] http://www.theblaze.com/stories/2012/03/19/jimmy-carter-on-homosexuality-jesus-never-said-a-word-about-it/

them from the beginning made them male and female, and said, 'Therefore a man shall leave his father and his mother and hold fast to his wife, and they shall become one flesh'? So they are no longer two but one flesh. What therefore God has joined together, let not man separate."

They said to him, "Why then did Moses command one to give a certificate of divorce and to send her away?" He said to them, "Because of your hardness of heart Moses allowed you to divorce your wives, but from the beginning it was not so. And I say to you: whoever divorces his wife, except for sexual immorality, and marries another, commits adultery."

The disciples said to him, "If such is the case of a man with his wife, it is better not to marry." But he said to them, "Not everyone can receive this saying, but only those to whom it is given. For there are eunuchs who have been so from birth, and there are eunuchs who have been made eunuchs by men, and there are eunuchs who have made themselves eunuchs for the sake of the Kingdom of Heaven." (Matthew 19:1–12)

When enemies of Jesus approached him about marriage—they were hoping to trick him into denying the authority of the Scriptures—Jesus successfully upheld marriage (Genesis 2:18–24) and the rest of Moses' words. In his defense of marriage and Moses, Jesus spoke in two places against all forms of sexual immorality. (Incidentally, Jesus' reference to Genesis 2 and his support for the rest of Moses' words show that he was in agreement with all the Old Testament. Jesus' agreement with the Scripture would also include Mosaic passages, like Leviticus 20:13, that speak against homosexuality.)

When Jesus said that sexual immorality destroys marriage—meaning any sexual activity among people outside of marriage—this included homosexuality. Homosexuality can only exist outside of marriage. According to Genesis 2 and all the Scriptures, marriage is only between one man and one woman. There is no marriage for same-gender couples in God's eyes, even if marriage exists for them in the eyes of people or in the eyes of the government.

As a side note, one of the reasons sexual immorality dissolves a marriage is found in the symbol or meaning God attached to sexual activity. Intercourse is a symbol of two becoming one, which the very act simulates. Sex is a sign of marriage (1 Corinthians 6:16). This is one critical reason why sexual activity outside of marriage is a sin. Sexual immorality suggests a union between people that God didn't make and doesn't acknowledge. At the same time, this mock union breaks a bond that God *did* make and desires to sustain between married couples. It also threatens any potential marital union that God may create between the unmarried.

Jesus' other words against sexual immorality in Matthew 19 come under his reference to eunuchs. Since Jesus showed from the Scripture that marriage is to be a permanent arrangement between one man and one woman, and because one cannot get a divorce for any and every reason before God, he pointed out that some people have turned away from marriage altogether. It's not by accident he calls them eunuchs (nonsexual people). Why does he call them that? Because the practice of human sexuality is a sign of marriage. Therefore, in his reference to "eunuchs," he was teaching us that those who don't marry are to give up all forms of sexuality with others. Jesus speaks against homosexuality with this reference as well.[12]

Born Again

Though you say you were born gay and, as such, confess that you are spiritually stillborn through natural birth—just as all of us are spiritually stillborn—did you know that you and I can be changed?

---

[12] There is yet a deeper reason that Christ guards chastity/purity (sexuality) under the institution of marriage. Marriage figuratively pictures the relationship between Christ and his church.

Did you know that everyone can be changed? We can. In fact, God wants us to change. This is what he has always desired for us since our fall into sin through our first parents (Genesis 3:15).

Here's a human argument to give evidence to this truth: We all can become anything we want to, right? Isn't that what people tell their kids from early on? Isn't change possible in all of us? Surely gender preference isn't an exception to the rule. It would seem unfair not to have a choice in that matter, wouldn't you agree? Don't people have that choice? Are they not permitted to choose a different way? I wouldn't dare suggest to any gay persons that they are incapable of loving or marrying someone of the opposite gender. If someone was to suggest that gay people can't love straight people, I'd honestly be curious to know why that is. What is there about people of the opposite gender that makes them unlovable, especially since God designed us to love them? It couldn't possibly be because of something as superficial as body parts, could it? If not that, then, in all seriousness, what is it? Don't let anyone fool you into thinking that you can't change, even if you are born a certain way. Who is anybody to tell you that you have to be stuck with who you are?

Here's another argument that I think emphasizes how much of a sinner I am—and that everyone else is too. You are not different or strange because of your same-sex attraction, though you might feel that way at times. Can I be honest with you about something? I admit it. I can change. I could become gay in my lifestyle—if I listened to and followed the world and all the desires of my sinful human heart. If you are looking for honesty from a Christian—and a pastor at that—it doesn't get more honest than what I'm confessing to you. However, because God forbids this condition and lifestyle, I refuse to pursue this sin willfully—or any other sin, for that matter. (By the way, if people say they are above this sin or any other, they don't know their capacity as sinners. They don't know the Scriptures as they should.[13])

---

[13] This truth of our absolute depravity is the reason for the popular Christian saying: "But by the grace of God, there go I."

Dear temple of God, I don't want to sin in any way, and I struggle not to (Genesis 39:9b). I want to show love to my Savior, so I choose to put away sin as surely as Jesus died to save me from it. That's the choice my Savior gave me through faith in him, and I'm glad for it. It's the same choice he's given to all who are in him through faith, and that, I believe, includes you. You and I can both change. Let's just choose not to sin willfully by Christ's strength. The Bible says that someone who is a Christian and struggles with same-sex attraction can learn all the more to say no to that form of ungodliness (Titus 2:11–12).

Don't mistake me when I say that you can change in Christ. I don't doubt that this would be a struggle for you, a struggle that you might argue I can't possibly understand. (Don't forget that I too am a sinner, no different from you.) And in no way am I saying that, with a change in mind-set, the struggle will abandon you. I'm afraid that the struggle over this will most likely remain with you for the rest of your life. I can't emphasize that sobering truth with you enough. This looks like it will be your lifelong thorn and cross. I would dare to say that some days will be far harder than others, even if you should increase the fight.

However, the struggle is worth it, and we must plead with the Lord to make the struggle ever less of a burden as time goes on. We must trust above all that he will not let anything burden us beyond *what he can handle* in his grace (1 Corinthians 10:13). And we must help one another carry each other's burdens (Galatians 6:2). That's what the Church is for.

Dear temple of God, it all really comes down to this question: do you believe you can be something new, and do you want to be whatever God wants you to be? Then let me encourage you to change accordingly. We can change through Christ. It may be difficult. It may feel impossible, but with God all things are possible[14] (Matthew 19:26; Philippians 4:13).

---

[14] Free will: many believe we have the ability to choose and do whatever we want. In regard to spiritual things like being born again, this is not the case. Our will is not free to choose in the things of God. Our will is in bondage to sin. Just as

Rainbow Savior

In fact, it's for this very possibility of the miraculous change of rebirth that the Bible was written and that Jesus came into this world. God created that book and sent his Son to accomplish the impossible and to change you and me—to change us all.

We should always see the Bible as a sign to us that something is wrong with you and me and all people, and that a change is needed. It's a holy book, and we are not holy. Its very presence teaches us that we have a fatal flaw, as do all people. This is precisely why that book was written.

But the same holy book is also proof that God won't give up on any of us as long as we breathe. All the Scriptures hang on this truth. In the pages of Scripture, played out in real human history, we find that God has done something about how we were originally born. He intends to use the holiness explained in the Bible not to condemn us but to save us. This book is here to make us holy. It is here to save us from the consequences of being born sinful as it communicates the message of Jesus.

We should think the same thing about change when we consider Jesus. He is here to hate the sin but to love the sinner.[15] He is here to eradicate our former selves. He's here to make you and me all brand-new. When we see his cross, we should see God's hatred for

---

we did not choose to be born physically or to be born into sin, so we can't choose to be born again. This change is a miraculous work of God alone, as it is taught in John 3 and other places (John 1:13; 15:16). The good news is that God desires to work this change in everyone through faith in Jesus Christ by the sending of his Spirit (John 3:5). Once we're born again spiritually, we receive the ability to exercise free will spiritually and do what's right, although we will never be able to do this perfectly on this side of heaven. Living for Christ comes with much struggle and much failure. Thanks be to God that he gives us the victory in Christ nevertheless (Romans 7:25–8:1)!

[15] It is true that God loves the sinner but hates the sin. At the same time, it is not true. Sinners who forever reject God's love will one day be rejected by God himself. Sometimes God rejects hardened sinners even in this life as he did with Pharaoh in the Old Testament (Exodus 9:12). Sinners can become the object of God's hatred while they live. People can get to a point where God will not distinguish them from their sin. All sinners should take to heart the seriousness of their sin and flee from it.

what we've been born into and what we've become in our sin. We should also see the damnation coming for us if we don't change. At the same time, we should see his unconditional love, offered in absolute forgiveness to change all that. We should move on to see in his resurrection from the dead a different life to live (Luke 24:45–47).

This hope of being born again is what Jesus grants to all who trust in him. Consider the real possibility of rebirth, which is yours already and which you can still live out. We find Jesus' teaching about rebirth and what it means in John 3:5–8, 15–21.

> Truly, truly, I say to you, unless one is born of water and the Spirit, he cannot enter the Kingdom of God. That which is born of the flesh is flesh and that which is born of the Spirit is spirit. Do not marvel that I said to you, "You must be born again."[16] The wind blows wherever it pleases. You hear its sound, but you cannot tell where it comes from or where it is going. So it is with everyone born of the Spirit.
>
> No one has ever gone into heaven except the one who came from heaven—the Son of Man. Just as Moses lifted up the snake in the wilderness, so the Son of Man must be lifted up, that everyone who believes may have eternal life in him …
>
> For God so loved the world, that he gave his only Son, that whoever believes in him should not perish but have eternal life. For God did not send his Son into the world to condemn him. Whoever believes in him is not condemned, but whoever does not believe is condemned already, because he has not believed in the name of the only Son of God.
>
> And this is the judgment: the light has come into the world, and people loved the darkness rather than the light

---

[16] Notice that Jesus was talking about the need for rebirth long before anyone started justifying themselves in saying, "I was born that way."

because their works were evil. For everyone who does wicked things hates the light and does not come to the light, lest his works should be exposed. But whoever does what is true comes to the light, so that it may be clearly seen that his works have been carried out in God. (John 3:5–8, 15–21)

May the Spirit of God come your way and mine all the more! May we hear the sound of the wind blowing (Acts 2:1–41), and may the Spirit effect change in our hearts once again! May our hearts ever flat line as to the darkness of our first birth, and may they ever beat again in the victorious light of the second birth! Though born one way, temple of God, we were meant to be born again. You have been born again.

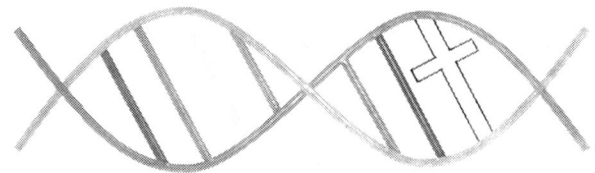

5

Embracing True Identity

Who Are We?

"Why can't you just accept me for who I am?" I wonder how many times words like that have been spoken over a kitchen table, on a car ride, or on a park bench from one relative or friend to another—a son to a father, a daughter to a mother, a friend to a Christian. Those are words spoken against an adverse reaction to a new and unwelcome identity. I wonder what it was like for you when you spoke those words to the people who care for you most, people who care about you more than all the other people in the world.

So you are gay, and this is your new identity. Admittedly, it's not an easy identity to accept, and that's for a number of reasons. That being the case, let's continue on with our discussion in this section about your new identity, your identity of being gay. This is really an extension of the previous chapter as surely as birth gives way to identity.

I would like to respectfully ask you, "Is that who you really are? Are you sure you are really gay?" Is it possible you could be wrong about that, even if you feel you couldn't be anything else? Honestly, who of us hasn't been wrong at times about something, even though we were sure we were right? Wouldn't the loving thing be, at least, to put that claim under the deepest scrutiny? After all, we're talking about your identity here.

As we set out to examine who you are, along with everybody else's identity, this demands patience all the way around. It's too important not to exercise patience with each other as we evaluate the claim being made. For instance, if one of my children claimed to be Superman and proceeded to climb onto the roof, ready to fly, wouldn't love compel me to say, "Hold on, dear child. Is that who you really are? Let's at least think this thing through before you jump!"? I would hope my child would have the patience to hear me out. Parental love would not say, "What can I do? It's who you are!" Love surely wouldn't say, "Aim for the stars! Go ahead and fly!"

Shall we see who you and I really are as to our true identities?

True Identity

Originally, God made us in his image. That's another way of saying that he made us after his own "identity" of holiness. The fact that we were made in the way of this image is reflected any time we refer to ourselves as "children of God." When I call you "dear child of God," as I often do in my preaching, I am speaking in reference to your relationship with your heavenly Father, which has been forged by grace. I am speaking to our purposed identity, whether we recognize it or not.

Sadly, back in the time of Adam and Eve, we lost the image of God, as is evident from our last chapter, which spoke about our sinful birth into this world. Being sinful is not reflecting the image of God's holiness. God did not create us to bear an unholy image. It was not his design that we would be "born that way."

In two important places early on in the book of Genesis, the Bible reveals that we had God's image and then lost it. At the creation of our race, God said, "Let us make man in our image, after our likeness" (Genesis 1:26). This was a conversation within the mystery of the triune God. Several chapters later, after the fall of humankind (Genesis 3), we read about our loss of God's image: "This is the book of the generations of Adam. When God created man, he made him in the likeness of God. Male and female he created them, and he blessed them and named them Man when they were created. When Adam had lived 130 years, he fathered a son in his own likeness, after his image, and named him Seth" (Genesis 5:1–3). After the fall into sin (Genesis 3), Adam's descendants were all born differently from the way they were originally created. This is true up to the present day. We all are born with an unholy identity in Adam's fallen "likeness."[17]

Because of the loss of the image of God, we find later on in the Bible that God sent his own Son into the world to restore his image to us. In Ephesians 4:24–25 we read, "Put on the new self, created after the likeness of God in true righteousness and holiness." Colossians 3:9–10 further explains, "You have put off the old self with its practices and have put on the new self, which is being renewed in knowledge after the image of its creator."

The whole concept of our old and new identities runs throughout the Scriptures from beginning to end. These identities also run throughout the many doctrines to which Christians hold, doctrines that you learned from early on. One could argue that all Christian doctrine addresses the old and new identities in some way, whether directly or indirectly.[18] Allow me to point out two prominent examples of Christian doctrine that speak to our old and new identities:

---

[17] This doctrine of original sin points to the need for the Savior to be born of a virgin. Jesus had to be born of a human being through an unnatural way so as not to inherit Adam's sinful nature.

[18] These doctrines include the doctrine of the Holy Trinity, and especially the work of the three persons of the Godhead to save us; the doctrines of the Word, baptism, and Lord's Supper; and even the following minor doctrines (are there really any "minor" doctrines?) that speak directly or indirectly to a former sinful identity and a new holy one: the doctrine of Christian vocation, end-times doctrine, the teaching of the Antichrist, the doctrine of church fellowship, etc.

- The doctrine of justification: The central doctrine of Christianity declares us "not guilty" for Jesus' sake (justification). This proclamation nullifies all the eternal consequences of bearing the fallen identity, the worst of which is eternal death. People of the new identity (people with faith in Christ) receive all the blessings of Christ through this declaration. Those blessings include eternal life and abundant life right now in a life of forgiveness and righteousness, an inheritance which only those who bear God's holy image receive (John 3:16–18).
- The doctrine of sanctification: This teaching pertains to our response to God in his grace of granting us a new identity, his holy image. Sanctification is all about reflecting that new identity in our daily living and putting down our old identity—all out of love for God's grace and mercy (Romans 12:1–2).

In this last doctrine about holy living, there is another doctrine that emanates and serves well in highlighting the importance of embracing the new identity instead of the unholy one. This teaching also impresses on us the struggle involved in ensuring that the new identity triumphs over the old. The doctrine of sanctification includes something that Christians refer to as the doctrine of the cross.

The doctrine of the cross comes from Jesus' words to his followers as he taught them about the nature of true discipleship. Jesus said, "If anyone would come after me, let him deny himself and take up his cross and follow me" (Matthew 16:24). This was a call from Jesus to put down the old identity and persevere in the new identity.

Notice how difficult this struggle is. Notice that Jesus compares the struggle to crucifixion! Jesus did not say, "If anyone would come after me, let him pick up his picnic basket. He'll be living on Easy Street. I'll heal him of all his problems. I'll shower him with riches. And I will welcome him as he embraces his former life of sin." On the contrary, putting to death the old self will at times feel like being crucified. To you, denying your same-sex attractions and way of life may actually feel like you are literally dying and unable to breathe. Thanks be to God, though, that he gives us the victory, no matter how much we struggle (Romans 7:25)! Only let us not give up the struggle![19]

Just as we do not need to deny someone's claim that they were "born gay," so too we don't need to deny anyone's claim that they have a "gay identity." In fact, I am not even bothered if you or someone else tries to link this to your DNA, a "gay gene." I won't deny that about you, but you need to know that such an identity is a reflection of your old one, which is perishing.

As to a "gay gene," here's news for us all from the Bible about that: The old identity of the sinful nature is the "gay gene" people have been looking for. The Bible has been declaring that to you and me since the fall of humankind. How relevant the Bible is and has always been! If anything, we're finally catching up to what the Scripture has always been saying to us on the issue at hand!

Beloved of the Lord, everyone inherited the corrupted "DNA" traits of our first parents' fallen identity. We sin, we age, and we die, and none of that is the perfect DNA God originally gave us. We live now with a corrupted form, through and through. Scientifically, we have only begun to see how our sin corrupts us genetically. As we have made clear, the Bible has always been focused on giving us the new "DNA" of Christ, if you will, in place of our old, corrupted genes.[20]

---

[19] The following point can't be emphasized enough: someone who struggles with temptations of same-sex attraction—or any kind—will likely struggle, and struggle greatly, their whole lives through. The apostle Paul refers to such a lifelong temptation as a "thorn in the flesh" (2 Corinthians 12:7–11), which the Lord allows in his mercy to keep his people clinging to his strength and grace alone to deliver them. We should not encourage a "pray away the gay" mentality (Conversion/Reparative therapy), which, in the end, can only crush the soul. One cannot pray away the sinful nature or convert it. We need to be brutally honest with the fatal attraction we bear toward sin, an attraction that can only grow more intense the more we flirt with it and become entangled in it.

[20] Is there any evidence for a "gay gene"? In short, it's too complicated of a biological issue for researchers to isolate or attach sexual orientation to only one gene or a combination of genes. Researchers generally agree that there are many

Rev. William A. Monday

Sexual Identity?

Human history is all about God giving us one new identity in place of our fallen one.[21] That is unmistakably clear from the Scriptures. That being the case, it would be a great tragedy for an individual to settle for any identity other than what God desires to make of us. This surely includes identifying ourselves according to sexual preferences.

May I kindly ask what good it does for any persons to identify themselves according to their sexual desires? What positive aspects has this brought about for you, for me, or for anyone? For instance, how has such a thing not distracted us from other pressing matters in life? How has the present LGBT issue not divided people? Look what it has done to you and me. Has this sexual identity really brought us closer together and to the Lord, or has it moved us further apart? I'm not looking to offend anyone by saying this. I sincerely have these questions.

Precious child of God, I'm not looking to minimize the seriousness of this issue by saying that sexual identity shouldn't exist. I'm actually hoping to catapult us over the base topic of mere sexuality. I'd suggest that we are suffering so much heartache on all sides because we are adopting identities that aren't even valid biblically. Whatever side of the issue a person is on, just imagine for a moment if there were

---

complicated factors involved, including concepts of *nature* and *nurture*. Many on both sides are also fearful of the social and political consequences of drawing conclusions one way or the other: http://www.pbs.org/wgbh/pages/frontline/shows/assault/genetics/nyreview.html.

[21] The church phrase *sinner-saint* was coined because of the former and new identities. The historic Lenten practice of *the imposition of ashes* (Ash Wednesday) also exists because of this truth. The tangible practice of imposing ashes in the sign of the cross on the foreheads of parishioners reminds them of their new identity and their former one. The ashes remind all sinners that they are merely dust and ashes apart from the redemptive work of their Savior. The shape of the cross, however, reminds them that they are now children of God because of their Savior's sacrifice for them. This is a very rich practice of confession and absolution, a practice that I know you have truly appreciated from the days of your youth. Remember what it means!

no identities like *gay* or *straight*. I only feel compelled to use these terms in writing to you because everyone is so accustomed to them. If it were up to me, I wouldn't utilize or even acknowledge those identities in any way.

One could argue that the identity of sexual orientation not only causes division but also degrades us. What about the majority of the time when people are feeling no preference at all—while they're busy at work or school, or as they carry on with everyday activities? To identify you or anyone according to sexual preference at such times is to imply that sexual identity is, in some way, more important than other aspects of your life or the good you are accomplishing. Does it not matter as much that a firefighter saves someone's life? Does it matter more that the firefighter is gay or straight? How depraved has the thinking become in our society!

Arguably, labeling ourselves according to "sexual orientation" might very well be destructive. What about those who struggle with their sexual preferences due to curiosity or wayward feelings, or through no fault of their own? Would that, perhaps, describe you in some way? If so, are we dooming you and a host of others because society has bought into the idea of sexual identities and their irreversibility? By labeling people this way—by labeling *you* this way—could we be implying that there is no way you can change from what you are? In our society, are we telling you that you have no choice?

Would you mind letting me share with you a very brief history lesson? Did you know that the thought of sexual identity did not occur to people until the 1800s? Secular historian and philosopher Michael Foucault, at least, argued that such a thing was unheard of at one time. In one of his works, he pointed out that the term *homosexuality* didn't come about until the nineteenth century (*History of Sexuality*, Vol. I, Part II). Even then, when the term was first used, homosexuality wasn't an identity. It was a term that merely referenced a type of sexual behavior.

Please don't mistake what I'm saying. It's not that people didn't have same-sex desires before the 1800s. There's no denying that same-sex attraction goes back to the fall of humankind. However, in times past, sexuality didn't define us. Why do we feel we must define ourselves this way now?

Please excuse me for what I'm about to say. I do not wish to offend you or anybody. It's just that I see what this issue is doing to precious people like yourself, a person so many people care about, a person so loved in the Lord and full of so many gifts. I am really angry about this whole sexual identity issue. (I'm not angry at you or at people who have been persuaded to go along with this kind of thinking. I'm angry about what is being said and done and what is becoming of eternal souls. I guess I'm as passionate about this at times as anybody else is. If anything, I hope you see how much I care for you!)

Are we so depraved—please forgive me—that we let our sexual attraction to another person create our identity? Are we really defining ourselves by where we like to fix our body parts—whether eyes, lips, or whatever? Please tell me that this is not what we have become. Precious child of God, that is not who you are. I mean no disrespect to anyone. We are in this together—all of us. But doesn't it just seem perverse to define ourselves sexually? Maybe one day we will leave behind this kind of identity, an identity that is no real identity at all. At least, for the greater part of human history, it never was, nor do we find such possibilities in the Holy Scriptures.[22] Oh, the grief that sexual identity has caused for people on both sides of this issue!

---

[22] One might argue, "But we do refer to ourselves as having many identities: mother, wife, father, husband, single, child, Latino, Asian, doctor, grocer, male, female, etc. How can you say that people have only one true identity?" Though we may refer to these human descriptions as our "identities," they are truly not. In some cases, they are transitory stations we come to, or they are roles that we are given and look to fulfill as a way to live out our identity of being children of God in this world. In yet other cases, they are identities of our own creation. Consider Paul's words in Galatians 3:26–28 about the only *identity* God recognizes: "For in Christ Jesus you are all sons of God, through faith. For as many of you as were baptized into Christ have put on Christ. There is neither Jew nor Greek, there is neither slave nor free, there is no male and female, for you are all one in Christ Jesus."

Just Animals?

While we're on the topic of identities, there is one more that you and I should consider. There's another way that people have grown accustomed to identifying themselves in society, although people rarely, if ever, say it outright. We too easily consider ourselves mere animals.[23] We have even been known to point out behavior in the animal kingdom to justify behavior among people. That's only one of the problems with identifying ourselves as animals.

As to traits of the animal kingdom, it's been said that animals sometimes exhibit homosexual behavior, and that's a proven fact. (We can see quickly where an idea like that is headed. The observation turns into an argument to promote homosexuality among humans as natural.) If it's in nature, it must be natural for us—or so the reasoning goes.[24] Perhaps we ought to contemplate this line of thinking a little too.

---

[23] Identifying ourselves as part of the animal kingdom stems from accepting Darwin's *theory of evolution*. The trouble with putting faith in that theory is that it devalues the human race and opposes any necessary absolute standard for morality. Though it is true that the evolutionary theory is in conflict with God's Word—denying creation, denying sin, denying death as a consequence of sin, and refusing the need for a Savior from sin—these two previously mentioned problems that the theory imposes on society have nothing to do with religion. In devaluing our race and attacking a sense of morality, the evolutionary theory has always posed a real threat to the quality of life for the religious and nonreligious alike.

[24] In Romans 1:20–2:1, the apostle Paul pointed out that homosexuality is "unnatural." Those in favor of homosexuality look to qualify Paul's use of the word "unnatural" here, and they appeal to the animal kingdom and human reason to do so. The argument goes as follows: Since there is homosexual behavior in the animal kingdom, it must be natural for some animals, and if it's natural for some animals, it must also be natural for some humans. Therefore, Paul is saying that heterosexuals who act out in homosexual ways are acting in unnatural ways and are displeasing to God. Likewise, homosexuals who act out in heterosexual ways are also acting in unnatural ways and displease the Lord.

Here are some other ways of misinterpreting Romans 1 (and the same goes for 1 Corinthians 6:9–10 and 1 Timothy 1:9-11): sexual religious rituals were forbidden; this section of Scripture is irrelevant for other times and cultures; the issue is not of sexuality but of power over others in dominating sexually and

If the human race is a fallen race, is it possible that the animal kingdom also suffered some kind of fall with it? The Scriptures confirm this possibility as a fact when we read, "For the creation was subjected to futility, not willingly, but because of him who subjected it, in hope that the creation itself will be set free from its bondage to corruption and obtain the freedom of the glory of the children of God. For we know that the whole creation has been groaning together in the pains of childbirth until now" (Romans 8:20–22a). God subjected all of creation to "futility," allowing it to be bound to "corruption" until a new order comes for it in the end. The Scripture says that the animal kingdom is corrupted. That hardly makes it a model for the human race to emulate.

The corruption found in the animal kingdom is also why animals die just like we do. Though the Bible does not call animals moral beings like we are—they are not accountable for sin, since they are not obligated to keep the law—nevertheless, they die because of the curse of sin we brought on them. What we fallen humans brought into the world impacts all of creation. As we've discussed in other places, that curse is death and every kind of suffering. Our sin is the reason why everything is falling apart. Originally, everything was perfect (Genesis 1:31). After sin came, everything became cursed and in need of restoration (Genesis 3:14–19). That includes animals.

This corruption is also why animals not only die but get sick, suffer pain, and share in our violent behavior toward animals and humans alike. This curse, in fact, is why animals do far worse things to themselves, humanly speaking, than is common to human behavior. Eating one's own young is just one of a number of deplorable activities found among animals. Because of sin, it's literally a "dog-eat-dog" world in the animal kingdom. As to this kind of "animalistic" behavior, would any of us find such behavior acceptable among humans? Though "natural," we all would agree that there are things animals do that are entirely detestable among people. Among humans,

---

abusing sexuality. All these arguments go beyond the simple sense of the text of the Scripture and become invalid arguments for doing so.

some kinds of behavior common in the animal kingdom would be considered cruel and, interestingly enough, *inhumane.*

If we agree that there are things in nature that would be tragic for humans to emulate, how do we distinguish between what in nature would be good for us and what would not? Morally speaking, there are those who would agree that if people were to swap partners in life as often as animals do, this would be morally reprehensible. Another rule animals live by is "survival of the fittest," but the same rule for humans is ultimately destructive to our race. If we lived by "survival of the fittest," what would become of the poor, the sick, the elderly, and entire impoverished populations and nations? What would happen to the "golden rule," the accepted religious practice of putting others before one's own self? What would happen to a founding principle of our country that all are created equal? Who's to say that the rare instances of homosexual behavior among animals should not fall into this same category of what is wrong? Animal behavior is hardly proof that same-sex attraction is right for them or for humans. Ultimately, God's Word must determine whether or not any patterns found in the animal kingdom are fit for human behavior.

As to God's Word, I'd like to conclude our thoughts here with a section of Scripture on the Savior's view of us. It brings out the dignity we've been given as a human race, a dignity that far surpasses anything we could derive from the animal kingdom or sexuality.

> O LORD, our Lord, how majestic is your name in all the earth! You have set your glory above the heavens ... When I look at your heavens, the work of your fingers, the moon and the stars, which you have set in place, what is man that you are mindful of him, and the son of man that you care for him? *Yet you have made him a little lower than the heavenly beings and crowned him with glory and honor. You have given him dominion over the works of your hands; you have put all things under his feet,* all sheep and oxen, and also the beasts of the field, the birds of

the heavens, and the fish of the sea, whatever passes along the paths of the seas. O Lord, our Lord, how majestic is your name in all the earth! (Psalm 8, emphasis added)

Dear temple of God, you are not an animal. You are not to be defined according to your sexual preference either. You are much more than that! Therefore, we ought only to accept one another as to our true identity. We are either children of God for Christ's sake or we could be. We are nothing less. We are either restored in the image of God already, or we are meant to be.

We are the crown of creation! It isn't love to embrace any identity for ourselves or others other than the one God made for us. It's deceptive. It's degrading. It's dangerous. It destroys. How would accepting lesser identities—and false ones at that—be any different from allowing a precious child to believe he's Superman and fall off a roof to his death? True love compels me to embrace you only as you really are in the Lord!

6

The Diversity of Love

Gay Love

I don't doubt that you are in love with your partner. I won't question that. The questions we ought to be asking, however, are these: What kind of love is it? Is it true love? Could it be something else? With love as diverse as it is, we would do well to agree upon some terms for love. When we do, we will understand more clearly what gay love really is.

The Different Kinds of Love

In the English language, we don't do very well in distinguishing between the many shades of love. I attribute that to the fact that there's just one default word for all those diverse expressions: *love*.

People love long walks on the beach. They love their high school sweethearts. Who doesn't love ice cream and comfort food? We love our friends. We love our pets. Moms and dads love their children. Patriots love their country. Married people love their spouses. You and I love God. People even say that they can "make love."

It's obvious that the love spoken of in each of those scenarios is quite different from the other forms of love mentioned, and we haven't even touched on love for unlawful things. Some people love to get high. Some love to take life. Some only love themselves. What about *those* forms of love? Should we equate unlawful forms of love with true love?

Eros

Eros[25] is the Greek word for a certain kind of love we stumble upon as we "come of age." There are other names for it, but positively speaking, let me just say that eros is basically romance or romantic love. This is the kind of love that Jacob had for Rachel in the Bible when he first laid eyes on her and found her beautiful (Genesis 29:9–18). The Old Testament poetical book, Song of Songs, has *eros* running throughout the whole thing. I presume that you have eros for your partner.

If you are attracted by the looks of a certain someone, and you feel all warm inside as you walk along the beach, I'd call that eros. If you like to make believe that a little angel named Cupid—formerly a Greek god—goes around on Valentine's Day and pierces hearts with the arrow of love, or if you believe in love at first sight, or if you can recall cartoon characters like Pepe Le Pu who become love struck, I'd say that you have come across eros. If you look back fondly on those days with your high school sweetheart, long for how it was in the early days of your present relationship, or have even become cynical toward those who are hopelessly "in love," then, you guessed it, it's all what I would describe as eros. I'd suggest to you that eros is all over the place in our society today.

To sum up, I see eros' beginning as physical attraction. Its end goal is sexual fulfillment. That is not to say that all forms of eros are

---

[25] *Greek-English Lexicon of the New Testament and Other Early Christian Literature* (BAGD). This reference has been utilized for the basic definitions of *eros, philia, agape,* and *storge.*

necessarily sexual. It's simply to say that on the continuum of eros, sexuality enters early on.

Eros seems to be the love that drives many relationships in our society these days. This is the "chemistry" so many people seek in the hopes of establishing a lifelong relationship in marriage. Conversely, when this "loving feeling" is lost, relationships often end—marriages too. When eros goes, the "high" of love is gone, feelings grow cold, and loving emotions die. We can see why many are tempted to call it quits at this point. From early on, we come to believe that we can't control our feelings, change them, or bring them back. I'm not sure why that is. We do speak in terms of "learning to love" someone, don't we?

We should know that something as fickle as eros isn't true love—at least not in the Greek language of the Bible. Hopefully that's a relief to you. We need to know that a husband and wife can still love each other even if they do not feel attracted to each other. It almost sounds like blasphemy in our day and age to say that you can be in love without feelings, but it's true. Romantic love does not equal true love, nor is it the greatest kind of love, contrary to what our society often makes of it.

For example, who in our society would imagine people getting married for reasons other than romantic love? I'm sure there are very few. Many people think that it would be a tragedy, "a great sin," to suggest that marriage is possible for other reasons. This is why many of us can't understand other cultures which practice the ancient tradition of arranged marriages. We feel sorry for them, even though, by and large, they have a greater success rate for marriage. The global statistic for arranged marriages which end in divorce hovers around 6 percent.[26] Compare that to our society's divorce rate of around 50 percent for first marriages, 67 percent for second marriages, and 75 percent for third marriages.[27]

---

[26] http://www.statisticbrain.com/arranged-marriage-statistics/

[27] http://www.divorcerate.org/

Some people might argue that arranged marriages oppress women and are mere contexts for abusing them, or that it is not the ideal form of marriage. They may claim that it is old-fashioned. That very well could be the case. I'm not here to argue for or against arranged marriages. At the same time, I wonder what other cultures would say about our approach to marriage and its failure rate. My point is merely to say that eros is hardly everything. In fact, reality seems to be teaching us that those who base their relationships on romantic love have a slim chance of making it.

We would be far better off if we did not consider romantic love as the highest form of love. It just isn't. Infatuation, passion, chemistry—whatever you want to call it these days—doesn't constitute a truly loving relationship. Though an exciting part of it and perhaps what sparks a courtship, eros is not what makes a relationship work. It's not even an essential ingredient for true love. If anything, eros can serve as one of a few short-lived gateways to help us "find true love," if we don't abuse it. True love can still exist, still flourish, without eros. True love can even revive eros when it's lost. But eros can never bring about true love.[28]

As good as eros can be, it can also be just as destructive. Negatively speaking, eros is lust and sexual perversion. This is where our English word *erotic* and its negative connotation come from. Because of our sinful state, we can take eros and become sexually attracted to things we were never meant for.

Some can get to a point where they only objectify others. People can be filled with eros while they're looking at pornography. Those who hope for something more at the end of a date are dabbling in the darker side of eros. Some can be driven to stalk others and take advantage of them in what becomes molestation or rape. Others can become attracted to people of the same gender and desire them sexually. Even children, out of curiosity, can stumble upon eros

---

[28] So as not to be misunderstood, God does intend for married couples to not only enjoy true love but to enjoy the gift of eros in a holy way. Still, eros is not equal to true love.

and persuade other children to do the same. But perhaps the most damaging thing of all is to think that eros will make you happy or make a relationship work.

The troubling thing about eros is that it is so powerful. People can be overcome by eros and get to a point in life where they feel like they are at its mercy. They can feel as if they have no control over it. The chemical reactions in the body, when eros takes over, have been compared to that same kind of craving that a cocaine addict has for another fix or that a compulsive gambler has for another hand of blackjack.[29] No wonder people can be so inclined to define themselves and their preferences by eros.

As an American people who are fueled by eros, it is critical to understand its nature. If only we could master it! If only we could learn to utilize it as it should be used and keep from turning it into the curse it often becomes!

Philia

Philia is another Greek word for love. I'd describe this very simply as the kind of love found among friends. Positively speaking, we can think of companionship. Philadelphia, the city of brotherly love, draws its name from this Greek word and another joined to it: *adelphos*. *Adelphos* means "brother."

After Jesus' resurrection, when Peter realized he could not offer true love to the Lord—he had denied Jesus three times the night before Jesus was crucified—a humbled Peter promised his Lord the next best thing. Peter offered *philia*, brotherly love (John 21:17).

Philia is when a couple of fifty years says of one another, "I married my best friend." Philia seems to be the kind of love that people hope underpins eros in a lifelong relationship in marriage.

---

[29] http://men.webmd.com/features/is-pornography-addictive. Addiction can signify change in brain structure: http://www.psychologytoday.com/blog/ending-addiction-good/201302/neuroplasticity-and-addiction-recovery.

However, when similar interests dissolve, when people go their separate ways, when they have nothing in common anymore, this too fails. Label it "irreconcilable differences," but in reality, these relationships ended because there was no more philia there.

Again, we can see why many would call it quits in such a situation. If a couple can't even enjoy friendship, why would the two stay together and make each other miserable? Philia, as great as it is, isn't the highest form of love. It's not true love. Though it runs deeper than eros and, as such, often lasts longer, it doesn't constitute a truly loving relationship.

Though it enriches love and is often thought of as the heart of love, philia too is not essential for true love. True love can still exist, still thrive, without companionship. As is the case with eros, true love can revive philia, never mind the extent of the brokenness that is there. But philia can never bring about true love.[30]

Philia can be destructive too. Since it's more of a love from the intellect than the emotions (eros), it can turn a relationship into a reasonable fifty/fifty contract between people. At this point, couples or friends can reason with each other that "as long as you scratch my back, I'll scratch yours." From my experience in pastoral counseling, when people begin thinking like this in a relationship, it's actually a sign that things are beginning to crumble. If something doesn't change, the relationship will eventually break. Expectations from one person begin to increase, while one's own failures are minimized in his own eyes: "She wasn't keeping her end of the bargain, so why should I?"

Negatively speaking, philia leads into forms of destructive behavior like becoming too controlling, obsessive, or needy. When philia is all there is, and it becomes too lopsided, one or both people in a relationship can lose their love for that friendship.

---

[30] Again, so as not to be mistaken, God does intend for married couples to not only enjoy true love but to enjoy *philia* and *eros* in a holy way. Those three gifts together are to make up a perfect marriage. True love is by far, however, the most important gift of love for marriage.

I fear that we also struggle to utilize philia properly in our American culture. In our "me-centered" society, we often view others as if they are here to serve us. In our relationships, we also seem to put much weight on common interests. Often these are as shallow as favorite pastimes. If only we would strive to make stronger and deeper connections with friends beyond that of entertainment, money, or travel!

We have much room for improvement in understanding philia. It's a love that allows us to be friends to others more than they befriend us. That's how it should be with friendship love.

Agape

Agape is the Greek word for true love. It stems neither from emotion nor the intellect. It comes from the will. It is a resolve to love, and that resolve never turns back. It doesn't permit the object of its affection to dissuade it either. Furthermore, the object of true love cannot cause true love to grow any more than it already has; true love is infinite in size already.

Paul, the apostle, described true love in 1 Corinthians 13. Arguably, it is the greatest chapter on love that has ever been written.

> If I speak in the tongues of men and of angels, but have not love, I am a noisy gong or a clanging cymbal. And if I have prophetic powers, and understand all mysteries and all knowledge, and if I have all faith, so as to remove mountains, but have not love, I am nothing. If I give away all I have, and if I deliver up my body to be burned, but have not love, I gain nothing. Love is patient and kind; love does not envy or boast; it is not arrogant or rude. It does not insist on its own way; it is not irritable or resentful; it does not rejoice at wrongdoing, but rejoices with the truth.

Rev. William A. Monday

> Love bears all things, believes all things, hopes all things, endures all things. Love never ends. (1 Corinthians 13:1–8)

Notice that there is not a word about romance (eros) in this section. Notice too that there's no talk about a fifty/fifty friendship (philia). In fact, the definition of true love according to 1 Corinthians 13 says that it's ready to sign a contract that is zero/one hundred. People who truly love, sign their lives away for another, demanding nothing in return. It's a love so great that it will offer itself whether or not the object of its affection ever responds to it. "Love bears all things." This love is divine (1 John 4:10, 16).

Enter Jesus Christ. If you want to see a picture of true love, all you need to do is look to the cross of Jesus. There, Jesus was dying for a people who hated him. There he was dying for a whole world of people who nailed him to a tree by their sin. Yet listen in: the first word Jesus spoke from the cross was nothing but love—true love. Jesus said of his enemies in prayer, "Father, forgive them for they know not what they do" (Luke 23:34). That's turning the other cheek to the nth degree. If there was anybody who practiced what he preached, it was Jesus, and no one preached love like he did (Matthew 5:38–42).

Listen to some of the other words Jesus spoke from the cross. You'll hear true love again, a love of divine strength. He provided for his mother, who was standing nearby, by giving her to John, his disciple whom he loved.[31] He said, "Woman, behold, your son!" (John 19:26). See how he did not for one instant think of himself! Even with his own death, he thought, "My mother is losing a son. I will see that she has another." He could only think of others and their need, never

---

[31] "Whom he loved" is a phrase some have picked up on as indicating that Jesus himself was gay. However, the Greek word utilized with this phrase is *agape*. It has nothing to do with sexuality (eros). I am, therefore, saddened deeply that such thoughts could ever be suggested about our Lord and Savior, especially as he hung stretched out on the cross to win salvation for all of us. Such thoughts are not born out of the Scriptures but out of an age and society that is, in my opinion, oversexualized. It seems we can hardly think of love apart from sex. This should not be.

Rainbow Savior

mind his own. That's true love. To another man being crucified, Jesus promised, "Today you'll be with me in paradise" (Luke 23:43). What a promise to one who didn't deserve it! This criminal had earlier mocked Jesus. Why would Jesus return love for hate? This murderer certainly couldn't benefit Jesus in any way. Why would Jesus even care for him? True love is the only answer.

In another word from the cross, Jesus said, in reference to his sacrifice for all our sins, "It is finished!" That is to say, "All their debts of sin are paid in full!" (John 19:30). There again is true love. Why would he pay the debt of our sin, sin that he didn't commit? Why would he spill all his lifeblood for a people who couldn't care less? Why would he suffer absolute torment for a people who like to define love any way but the way he showed us on the cross?

Look a little closer at the cross of Jesus. Though he could have taken himself off the cross at any time (John 10:17–18), he stayed there so that all of his enemies, which included you and me, might be saved (Philippians 2:6–11). His enemies obviously thought there was no one weaker than this man from Nazareth. They taunted him to come down, figuring that he was powerless to do so (Matthew 27:40). Looks, however, can be deceiving. If only they had known that he was doing all of this out of love for them, the loveless. True love, however, is never obvious to people who don't know what it really is. Dear temple of God, are you still able to recognize what true love looks like and what it doesn't, even as you read through these pages? I pray that you are still able.

As we see Jesus on the cross, let me ask you: Do you see a speck of eros there? Do you even see a hint of philia? There's only agape.[32] There's only true love. There's not a warm feeling toward us to keep him going. There's not any intellectual reasoning or companionship to convince him to stay crucified. There is only his act of will to show

---

[32] This is not to say that agape is void of feelings or reason. But when there is no cause for warm feelings or a pleasing reason to continue on with another person, agape (commitment) perseveres in the hope that warm feelings and pleasing reason might one day be established.

love to an object of his affection, an object that—try as hard as we will—cannot dissuade him from loving us.

At the cross was a love that literally suffered hell and came back for us. There was a love that remained unbroken. This is the love talked about in Romans 5:8: "But God shows his love for us in that while we were still sinners Christ died for us" (Romans 5:8). That's the love referred to in 1 Corinthians 13. It's the only love that can make a relationship last. Even the grave cannot end the relationships of those born of such love (Romans 8:38–39).

True Love Is for Everybody

We could talk about more forms of love, but in the end, nothing compares to agape. Nothing. Not even a mother's love (*storge*) can rival agape, as strong as a mother's love may be. A mother's love can fail, but true love never fails. Isaiah shared the awesome nature of true love compared to a mother's love when he quoted the Lord saying, "Can a woman forget her nursing child, that she should have no compassion on the son of her womb? Even these may forget, yet I will not forget you. Behold I have inscribed you on the palms of My hands" (Isaiah 49:15–16). God won't ever forget us, especially those who believe. He carved out the memory of us deep within his hands by some Roman nails fixed in a cross. This is the kind of love we all are looking for in our relationships.

Can you imagine friends having that kind of love as a foundation for philia? And what about married couples? Not one relationship would break. Can you imagine if this love came first, before eros? There would be no pornography. There would be no extramarital teenage pregnancies. There would be no sexuality outside of marriage. No woman would ever be raped. No child would ever be molested. There would be no infidelity among the married either. Even more, can you imagine if this love of agape took the place of all our hatred in the world? There'd be no more wars among nations, only peace. There'd be no more issues of any kind.

God doesn't want to keep true love from those who call themselves straight. He doesn't want to keep true love from those who call themselves gay either. He doesn't want to keep it from those who are Christian or those who are not. Jesus died for everybody. He did this so everyone could have true love. Know then that this love of the will is waiting for you in Christ at his cross. It always is. This is the love that overrules our emotions and intellect. At the same time, it's a love that miraculously enables eros and philia to submit to the will of God gladly. It makes no difference who you are. It makes no difference where you come from. It makes no difference what preferences you have. True love is yours through faith in Christ, and it's yours to rule over all forms of love in submission to Christ.

God truly wants everyone to have this love. This is why he made us in the first place. This is why he redeemed us in the second place. This is why he won't give up on us in the third place—not for as long as we live.

The Love Misplaced

Let's return now to the topic of gay love, the love you have for your partner. I've heard it said from those in favor of homosexuality, "Who would ever want to keep someone from loving another human being?" That argument strives to cut to the heart of the matter. It looks to render any sentiments against gay love as absurd.

Would it surprise you that I agree with the argument? The answer to that question should always be an absolute, "Nobody! Nobody should want to keep love from anyone else! No one worth listening to should want to keep anyone from loving another person!" I surely don't want to keep anyone from experiencing true love. Most importantly, the Bible, which states that "God is love," doesn't either. People who argue that all people should be loved truly do care.

The trouble is that we're not talking about true love or even brotherly love when we're talking about gay love. That's the bottom line. This is the whole issue. With all due respect, people who argue in support of homosexuality by saying it's about true love are misguided. Gay love is not about true love. It's not even about companionship. Gay love is about eros.

True love shared will never make you gay or straight. Companionship, at the deepest level of brotherly love, won't make you gay or straight either. And these forms are allowed by God for you and your partner. But love for the same gender in regard to eros is what makes one gay, and this kind of love is unlawful according to the Scriptures. So the whole issue of gay love comes down to sex and sexual attraction. Think about that for a moment as we review the diversity of love.

The Bible wants two men or two women to share true love, agape love, with each other. In the section we just read, Jesus said that he has true love for everybody. He is committed to us all unconditionally. No matter what we do, his love will not fail us. There's no greater love than that the Savior would lay down his life for us (John 15:13). There's no greater love than commitment, an act of the will. Two men, two women—*anybody* can share that kind of love. In fact, there is no other way. I am not against true love between anybody. Neither is the Bible. But remember that true love has nothing to do with eros.

The Bible also wants two men or two women to share in true friendship, philia. Think of David and Jonathan in the Old Testament. They shared brotherly love and enjoyed one another's companionship. They were closer than brothers (1 Samuel 20:17). They had everything in common. David scratched Jonathan's back, and Jonathan scratched his (1 Samuel 20:38–42). Their love was true love too! For David, the friendship he shared with Jonathan was greater than the friendship love he ever experienced with any woman, even if such a woman was called his wife (2 Samuel 1:26). Two men, two women—anybody can share that kind of love, a love that is never sexual. There is to be no other way. I am not against brotherly love between anybody.

Neither is the Bible. But remember that brotherly love has nothing to do with eros.

Gay love is a misuse of eros. It's a love, but it's a love that is misplaced. This is why it's a sin. Interestingly enough, all sin can be defined as love misplaced.[33] The Bible defines sin that way, for it directs us to where our love should be placed: toward God and our neighbor as defined by God's law (Matthew 22:36–40). Anything else is rebellion against God. It's misplaced love.

Dear temple of God, I do not write this to shame you. I write this because I care. I write this because anyone who abuses a blessing from God can only turn it into a curse. God doesn't want his blessing of sexuality to become a curse for you, your partner, or any of us. In the hope of keeping sexuality as a blessing for you and me and all God's people, I'd like to end this section with a prayer to the God who alone can preserve love in all its holy forms and, in that, can save us all:

Lord God, true love incarnate, don't give up on us as a people. Teach us, gay and straight alike, about the true diversity of love and what true love is. Help us to share your love with each other as surely as you never stop sharing it with us. May that love of the cross persuade us to put sexual attraction and sex in its proper place—back in the marriage chambers and out of the public square and every other aspect of our lives! Help us to understand that sex is not love, nor is it our life. Help us to see that it's a sacred gift to be shared between one man and one woman for noble purposes, which you alone designed for marriage. Then, let true love and friendship reign among us all as we strive to put eros back in its proper place. Let this be to your glory for the sake of precious souls who are often confused about the true diversity of love. Amen.

---

[33] A concept from St. Augustine's *Confessions*.

7

The Happy Lifestyle

"I wouldn't have chosen this life, if I had a choice. Nobody chooses to be gay." I can't get those words out of my mind, words that you said to me some time ago. It's pretty clear that you aren't happy in what you are and in what you have become. For whatever reason, from your own words, it's clear that being gay is not the happy lifestyle you were looking for.

Is this unhappiness due to not being accepted by everybody? I get the sense that you believe that is the reason. But could it be something more? Believe me when I say I only want you to be happy, truly happy. My words to you are a sign of that. I am not here with any desire to make you miserable. I know you know that.

Gay Means *Happy*?

It's interesting to me that at one time the word *gay* had a first definition of "happy." That seems to be the case for the early 1960s and several decades prior.[34] Because of our modern-day use of the

---

[34] In the early twentieth century, there was a fascination in pop culture with the 1890s and what became known as the "Gay Nineties." This trend, which romanticized that time period, had nothing to do with homosexuality. It did,

word, this primary understanding has slipped down a few spots in the word's meaning. Now the first definition is, of course, homosexual.

In the hope of seeing you truly happy, let's return to the definition of the word *gay* as it was used in the early part of the twentieth century (happy), and let's set out to answer one simple question: is the gay lifestyle a truly happy one, or is there a happier lifestyle above all lifestyles waiting for everybody?

Is it possible that there is still a lifestyle waiting for you where you can be happy in every way? Arguably, the matter is entirely subjective. At the same time, since the gay lifestyle is being purported among us as a perfectly happy one for some, yet apparently not for you, perhaps we can examine what God says makes people altogether happy.

The Source of Unhappiness

I can't help but think that your stress over your new lifestyle sounds a lot like the kind of stress the psalmist experienced when he was living contrary to God's design (Psalm 32). I realize that you may feel like your stress is a result of not being accepted by others, but I'm suggesting the source of your unhappiness is coming from a conscience that is crying out to you to conform to what God has ordained for you, a lifestyle that is quite different from your current one.

What I'm thinking of in particular is a biblical example of King David's life as described in Psalm 32:3–4. After King David fell into

---

however, give a new sense to the word *gay* that had connotations of loose living. From the early 1900s to the 1960s, *gay* became a word to express more of a happy, carefree, and euphoric way of living, which wasn't necessarily tied to wayward living. Popular songs like "Meet the Flintstones" (1962) and "Deck the Halls" (<1930) use the former meaning of the word *gay* in lines like "We'll have a gay ole time!" and "Don we now our gay apparel." These are lines which inevitably cause kids to laugh a little in more recent generations, because they are unaware of the change in meaning that occurred after 1960. (A look at the entire etymology of the word *gay* is, in my opinion, an interesting read.)

sexual immorality, he felt as you do now. At least his words seem to be communicating what you are expressing, in that you are not entirely happy. He wrote, "For when I kept silent, my bones wasted away through my groaning all day long. For day and night your hand was heavy upon me; my strength was dried up as by the heat of summer." I know many would suggest stress over homosexuality is all external, but according to the Scriptures, the overwhelming stress is internal. And, as with David, that stress can manifest itself in physical and external ways.

Dear temple of God, the Lord came to relieve you of your stress. Surely he has plans to prosper you and not to hurt you but to give you a future and hope in Christ (Jeremiah 29:11). So, what is his plan for you to be happy?

The Holy Lifestyle Is the Happy Lifestyle

Everyone has problems. We all have issues we have to deal with. It's not just you or gay people like you. It's all of us. We are all in this together. We are all looking for happiness, but it often eludes us when we look for it in the things of this life. Let me, then, share with you from the Scriptures the path to true happiness.

The great teacher from the Old Testament, King Solomon—wisest man of all, next to Jesus—can shed a little light on the way to happiness for us. In the book of *Ecclesiastes*, which he is believed to be the author of, we find this passage: "[God] has put eternity into man's heart, yet so that he cannot find out what God has done from the beginning to the end. I perceived that there is nothing better for [people] than to be joyful and to do good as long as they live; also that everyone should eat and drink and take pleasure in all his toil—this is God's gift to man." (Ecclesiastes 3:11b–13).

Our hearts will forever remain restless until we are found in God, living according to his design. Therefore, being found in God and keeping within his design is both the beginning of real happiness and the path to a happiness that can never end. This is his gift to all who receive Christ.

The Bible calls real happiness by another term. The word is not "gay." It's "blessed." The Scriptures call true happiness *blessedness.* The happy lifestyle, according to God, is the holy lifestyle. Consider that truth as the writer of Psalm 1 proclaims it.

> *Blessed* is the man who walks not in the counsel of the wicked, nor stands in the way of sinners, nor sits in the seat of scoffers; but his delight is in the law of the LORD, and on his law he meditates day and night.
>
> He is like a tree planted by streams of water that yields its fruit in its season, and its leaf does not wither. In all that he does, he prospers. The wicked are not so, but are like chaff that the wind drives away.
>
> Therefore the wicked will not stand in the judgment, nor sinners in the congregation of the righteous; for the LORD knows the way of the righteous, but the way of the wicked will perish. (Psalm 1:1–6)

Real joy is a life of holiness. I know what you might be thinking at this point: holiness doesn't seem like a lot of fun. If we're thinking holiness is hardly happy living, know that there is truly nothing more joyful than the holy lifestyle. If we can't imagine holiness as happiness, it's only because someone has pulled the wool over our eyes. The ancient deceiver who leads the world astray has been getting us to define happiness as anything but holiness. Let's not be deceived any longer. Holiness is what makes our spirits soar and our hearts sing.

Now, here's the beauty about the true God in regard to holiness. Did you know that he doesn't expect you to earn holiness? I think holiness seems undesirable to so many because we are told by practically everybody that we have to work for it, and for sinners, holiness is impossible to earn.

Here's the good news: God doesn't expect you to earn it, not even in part! He doesn't even expect you to be able to find it! He must lead us to it, and when we see it, he must earn it for us and declare us to be holy by grace. Holiness is a gift God alone gives to us. Holiness means being clothed in Christ's righteousness.

Precious temple of God, the Lord has already declared you to be holy in Christ, and through faith in Jesus you receive all the benefits of that holiness. Happiness is already yours! You may just not know it yet, or perhaps you've forgotten that truth. But when you can see again that God is taking care of everything, when you can see that all's forgiven, when you can see that you can leave all other paths for the narrow one of holiness, then you'll begin to feel the blessedness that God has already won for the world. At that time, his commands won't be so burdensome.

In due time, his yoke will be light (Matthew 11:30). Eventually, your heart will be free, and one day you'll feel like running in the path of his commands (Psalm 119:32). In seeing his love for you, his commandments to love him and love others will become like a candy shop where we, as his children, get to have our pick of his commands and taste them all (Psalm 119:102–105).

Now, don't get me wrong. Holiness doesn't necessarily mean an easy life—quite the contrary. Holiness often mean's suffering outward persecution and inward self-denial. But the holiness that God gives provides an internal happiness to weather every storm in life, from outside or from within. God's holiness ultimately provides an eternal joy in the fullest way, a way that is yet to come. As to the happiness of holiness and how it works, I'm reminded of Moses' life and the way the writer of the book of Hebrews describes it: "By faith Moses, when he was grown up, refused to be called the son of Pharaoh's daughter, choosing rather to be mistreated with the people of God than to enjoy the fleeting pleasures of sin. He considered the reproach of Christ greater wealth than the treasures of Egypt, for he was looking to the reward" (Hebrews 11:24–26).

Here's another blessing of holiness: through the truly holy lifestyle, God will renew those of us who have not fared so well in other ways of living, whether in body, soul, or mind. The complete restoration might not happen in this life. In God's infinite wisdom, not all the struggles and health issues of the body and soul will necessarily be resolved this side of heaven, but one day all things will be made new (Revelation 21:5). One day we who are in Christ's holiness will be made whole! One day beyond the grave, all who are covered in Christ's holiness will be healthy and happy unlike we could ever be in this life (Isaiah 40:30–31).

Dear temple of God, that's the happy lifestyle that is worth building your life around. This happy lifestyle lies right before you now in a community called the holy Christian church, which is the greatest community of all. Holiness waits for you to walk down its path once more. There is no greater cause to fight for than this holiness that comes in Christ by God's grace.

We can pursue true happiness together in the Lord, no matter how difficult the road seems at the start. Come back to the fold. Come back to the flock. What happiness you will experience and bring to your Savior, to his angels, to me, and to all God's people, when you return!

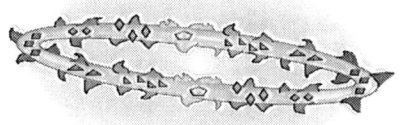

8

No Greater Friend

Dear temple of God, what more is there to say? Of course, if you want to continue on in this conversation and return to any points for more discussion, my door is always open to you. I will talk with you for as long as it takes—until our Lord comes or takes me home. But soon, all of this needs to come to a head. None of us are even promised tomorrow. As you consider, then, all of our Savior's words in what I've shared with you, please permit me to leave you with a couple of last thoughts.

No Greater Love

Once there was a precious American among many other Americans, all of whom decided, for whatever reason, to visit a foreign and hostile country. After some time in this other country, this gifted and loved American and all the others were surrounded by the authorities and taken in for questioning. They were all charged for crimes against the state, crimes worthy of death.

Sadly, there was no way out for these Americans. They all tried to argue that they were innocent of the crimes. They claimed that they were only there to visit in peace, to embrace the foreign culture and customs for a little while, and then to return home, intending no harm to anyone. But the evidence was stacked a mile high against them. Word even spread that these American citizens were guilty of treason against their own country. Their captors made such reports in the hopes that there would be no possible rescue from abroad. After facing the judge in the land of their doom, all were sentenced to die. All were facing the gas chamber. The hours began to wind down for them all.

As they were sitting together in their final moments, one hostage said to his fellow Americans, "I heard from the outside that there is someone who is coming to our defense, someone who can actually help us." Another one asked the inevitable question, "Who? Who is it?"

The hostage whispered, "I heard that an ambassador is coming from the president himself." A second American concurred, saying, "It's true. I also heard that the president is carrying out a plan to release us all through someone from his own inner circle. They say the ambassador is already on the way."

As they waited, the one precious, gifted, and loved American wondered if it could be true. The ruler of the land was crying out for their blood. Many wondered how the president's ambassador could satisfy a tyrant as evil as that. This doubt especially overwhelmed the thoughts of the one precious American. She said to herself, "Could this really be happening? Could there really be any way out of this mess and out of a country that only wants Americans dead? This must be a dream from which I just can't wake up."

Then, to her horror, some of those she'd thought were fellow Americans got up. They turned on the first hostage who spoke of rescue, and they killed him. The second prisoner, who had echoed his fellow American's words of hope, suffered the same fate by those traitors. As the criminals killed them both, the traitors shouted to all the others to declare allegiance to the enemy. They reasoned that this alone could be their only hope.

It was at this point that the one precious American realized that something far beyond her knowledge had been happening. They had

Rainbow Savior

all been set up. She even reflected on her own actions and realized that she was truly guilty of all the charges against her, although she did not realize what she had been doing at the time. Terrified in the darkness, she waited. Other Americans fell into despair. Many others declared allegiance to the enemy. Yet some refused to bow a knee and hoped against all hope.

Not too long after the two hostages were murdered, a solitary figure entered death row. It was just as the two Americans had said. There was an ambassador from the president. But she was dressed in the same prison clothes of all the American hostages. She had her number assigned to her, just as they all did. The captors even humiliated her as they took a mug shot so that all would recognize whom they had taken captive.

Shackled like everybody else—though guilty of no crime—she was led to her own cell apart from the others. Her captors raised the light over her, and no one could believe their eyes. Everyone was stunned. It was the president's own daughter. She had been sent to take the place of her fellow Americans. The plan was unfathomable.

A recording of the president's voice broke in over the crowd: "This is my child, whom I love. There is no one more pleasing. This is the sacrifice to set you free. Do everything my child tells you."

The girl looked like a dove in all her innocence. Upon her arrival, surprisingly, the guards gave the Americans back their clothes to wear, which they took, but none were permitted to leave their cells. The traitors shouted that the tyrant of the land was too strong to overcome—and now he had the president's own daughter! Some of the Americans realized that receiving their new clothes was a token of the freedom that was inevitably coming. The precious American didn't know what to make of that act. Regardless, the president's daughter began to proclaim the plan.

After sharing the message of how her father intended to free the hostages, the ambassador was allowed one last meal. It was her favorite meal. She also requested that everyone taken captive should be invited to share in it freely, trusting in the sacrificial work that she was about to carry out. This was to be a banquet to celebrate the freedom that was about to be delivered in full to all of them, whether traitor or captive.

Some ate. Some drank. The gifted American ate and drank a little and then stopped. She was being pulled in two directions. The hardened traitors refused to participate, as they had put their hope in the tyrant of the land. All who participated in faith did so in order that their lives would continue in freedom. The president's daughter also ate and drank, but it only prepared her for her death, which would set the others free. All of them realized, deep down—traitor and captive alike—that this meal transcended all others.

Finally, the supper ended. The ambassador cried out to see if there could be any other way the hostages could go free. There was no word of response from the child's father. The demand was that justice be served. It was clear to her that there was no other way. Someone had to pay the price for the guilt of all the hostages. It couldn't just be anybody either. It had to be somebody worth more than all the rest. The ambassador grew determined. She carried on with full resolve, and the precious American was a witness to it all.

The president's daughter was escorted to one last room, the gas chamber. To add insult to injury, the guards lifted up her picture before the other prisoners and spit on it. They mocked her with all sorts of insults and then tore the picture to shreds. All of the traitors cheered. The precious, loved, and gifted American didn't know what to do. Should she show allegiance to the one who was giving up everything for her? Or should she just blend in with the traitors?

As the traitors noticed her and her indecision, they began to surround her. They began to mock her and ridicule her for who she was and for any thoughts of devotion toward the ambassador that might be stirring inside. Amazingly, the ambassador spoke up for her and attracted and bore all the attention and insults for her.

Then the eyes of the president's own met the eyes of the one American. It was as if the president's ambassador was proclaiming, "Who else could ever love you like this? You have no greater friend than I." Finally, the president's daughter was restrained in the God-forsaken place of execution, and the door was sealed.

At that time, all the prison doors swung open. All were free to flee the country—even the traitors who had mocked the ambassador and murdered the others. Everyone stood in disbelief. It seemed as if three days passed before any prisoners made a move and put their faith in the sacrifice that had been offered up for them.

Suddenly, there was a great exodus of Americans. Many ran for freedom and would not stop until they had made it to their home country. In the streets, they proclaimed to everyone the great deeds of their leader and what he had given up for them. They could not help but speak. Many traitors, however, remained and sought to attack the other Americans as they fled. But the precious, loved, and gifted American was caught in the middle of it all. No one was quite sure what she would do.

Dear temple of God, you are the precious, loved, and gifted American in this story. I'm sure you recognized early on that this was all about you and Jesus Christ, who gave his life for you. Surely you connected all the dots between the story of your life and the one I just proclaimed to you.

Could you have a greater friend than Jesus? Who else has so loved you that before you were even born he sent the prophets ahead of you to proclaim hope for you in the captivity of your sin? Look what the sinful world did to those prophets, and yet Christ still loves us. See how he came, regardless of your treason and mine. See how he still seeks you in your present choices and indecision regarding him. Did he not clothe you in freedom and his righteousness in your baptism, even as he put on the filthy prison clothes of our sin when he stepped into the Jordan River to be baptized? Look at the humiliation he went through for your sake, so that you might be free and exalted. Did he not also give himself in the Holy Supper for your release from sin—miraculous food and drink that once passed over your lips?

Even now—as many in the world ridicule you, and the self-righteous turn on you and call you all sorts of things for your present choices—isn't he the one who turns all their attention and insults back on himself at the cross? Wasn't he the one who was bundled up together with all that was wrong, like sticks destined to be burned and consumed by the wrath of God on the cross—all in our place for your damnable sins and mine?

It was not you who suffered hell to set yourself free. It was not I. It was not any of those in the company you keep who claim to be your friends and who support you in your new lifestyle. It was Jesus alone who took your place of condemnation and mine. Don't the Scriptures say that he has "borne our griefs and carried our sorrows, yet we esteemed him stricken, smitten by God, and afflicted" (Isaiah 53:4)? Surely you can see him looking at you in his Word, proclaiming, "Greater love has no one than this, that someone lay down his life for his friends" (John 15:13).

No Greater Response

There's one more thought we need to remember concerning Jesus, his love, and the proper response due him for such love. Jesus, who was known for going out to the lepers and sitting down with tax collectors and prostitutes—the professional sinners of his day—once crossed paths with a woman who was desperate to be loved, truly loved, and no longer used. Though everyone else was disgusted by her, Jesus saw something more for her, as only he could.

> Jesus went to the Mount of Olives. Early in the morning he came again to the temple. All the people came to him, and he sat down and taught them. The scribes and the Pharisees brought a woman who had been caught in adultery, and placing her in the midst they said to him, "Teacher, this woman has been caught in the act of adultery. Now in the Law Moses commanded us to stone such women. So what

do you say?" This they said to test him, that they might have some charge to bring against him.

Jesus bent down and wrote with his finger on the ground. And as they continued to ask him, he stood up and said to them, "Let him who is without sin among you be the first to throw a stone at her." And once more he bent down and wrote on the ground. But when they heard it, they went away one by one, beginning with the older ones, and Jesus was left alone with the woman standing before him. Jesus stood up and said to her, "Woman, where are they? Has no one condemned you?" She said, "No one, Lord."

And Jesus said, "Neither do I condemn you; *go, and from now on sin no more.*" (John 8:1–11)

So, what now? Dear temple of God, let the love of Christ move you to return to the fold and save yourself from this wicked generation (Acts 2:40):

1. Recognize homosexuality as a sin, and confess it to the Lord.
2. Repent of sins committed.
3. Trust in the forgiveness offered and received. You are forgiven and loved!
4. Connect to God's Word, remember your baptism, and return to the Lord's Supper to strengthen your faith.
5. Strive to sin no more. Strive not to give in, and don't ever give up.
6. Seek support from fellow Christians and Christian counselors. I am here! I've always been here for you, and so have many others.
7. Pray ceaselessly for Christ's rescue, as I am doing for you.

Jesus said, "Greater love has no one than this, that someone lay down his life for his friends. You are my friends *if you do what I command you*" (John 15:13, emphasis added).

Part II

A Shepherd Reaches Out to His Flock

9

Welcome to Oz

Many among the LGBT community feel oppressed by the rest of society. Many of them especially feel oppressed by Christian people like you and me. There are a number of gay people who are hurt and angry about how they have been treated, especially as they feel that Christians are constantly plaguing them with thoughts about God and judgment over their lifestyle. All the while, they feel as if Christians are trying to keep them from enjoying certain freedoms in this country. When I consider this reality for them, my thoughts are drawn to some words from Ecclesiastes, which follow shortly.

As a congregation of believers, we might do well to begin our discussion—whether we are gay or straight—by considering why living our lives is so difficult. We can utilize the experience of having a hard life to engender in our hearts compassion for all who are gay. Then we will be more level-headed when reaching out to them.

We all have issues. We all have problems. The root cause is always the same: sin. Sin is in each of us, and it entirely corrupts us all. Therefore, we all can admit that we need to find rescue and that Jesus Christ is the only Savior. Let's spend a moment and talk about the source of all our problems, and while we're at it, let's be brutally honest about how we Christians, along with the rest of humanity, have contributed to the problems we have. Finally, let's be reminded again of what the only real solution is for any of us.

This Is Not Our Home

"I saw all the oppressions that are done under the sun. And behold, the tears of the oppressed, and they had no one to comfort them! On the side of their oppressors there was power, and there was no one to comfort them. And I thought the dead who are already dead are more fortunate than the living who are still alive. But better than both is he who has not yet been and has not seen the evil deeds that are done under the sun" (Ecclesiastes 4:1–3).

Why is life so hard that we sometimes wish we had never been born at all? Why do we have tsunamis that claim the lives of over 230,000 people in one fell swoop? Why do we have earthquakes that decimate entire countries—countries like Haiti, which are already impoverished? We live in fear of asteroids pummeling our planet and viruses ravaging our bodies. Sometimes it feels like our world is just a rag doll in a puppy's mouth. Nature keeps calling out to us that something is terribly wrong with this place (Romans 8:20–21).

Perhaps the worst hardships we encounter, however, are not what nature throws at us but what we often bring upon ourselves. How does it make any sense that fellow human beings would wrap themselves up in Al Qaeda garb and rip through World Trade Center towers by turning 747s into missiles? In the end, those terrorists accomplished only one thing: they killed their own kind, members of the same human race.

Why do we have shootings in parking lots, movie theatres, and kindergarten classrooms, where the innocent die at the hands of people as messed up as the massacres they make? How can a mother send her own babies to the bottom of a lake in a runaway car, or drown them in the shallow waters of a bathtub? How can people be beaten for the color of their skin? How can others be bullied over their sexual preferences? Sometimes it feels like we are living in a horror movie worse than anything Stephen King could imagine. We can hear the blood of all the slain crying out from the ground that something is terribly wrong with our race (Genesis 4:10).

There's no doubt about it. There's something wrong with the world. *There's something wrong with all of us.* This can't be how it was meant to be. This place—as beautiful and as messed up as Oz—can't be our home.

The Wicked Witches

Who's at fault for all the horror we face in this life? Would you mind if we played the blame game for a little while? I know that it's rarely, if ever, productive to lay blame, but I'm hoping in this case it might be of some good. Perhaps some gay people will be more open to talking with Christians if we are genuinely honest with them, which the Scriptures call us to be. Perhaps then we can begin to point them toward a solution for all the problems we face as a human race. For there is indeed one common problem that runs throughout it all: our sin. At the risk of making things worse—but in the hope of making things better—here comes the blame.

The Wicked Witches of the West and East

The first entity I'd like to point a finger at is the visible church on earth, the church we see.[35] Are you surprised? I hope not. It's not like she doesn't have her warts. I'm not the only one to notice that

---

[35] Theologians have made a distinction between the good, invisible church (holy Christian church) and the visible church on earth, which can be evil in part and can commit evil "in God's name." Church fathers as far back as St. Augustine (AD 300s–400s) have historically divided the visible church (what is seen as either good or bad) from the invisible church (which the Lord sees as truly and only good).

either. Who hasn't? There's a whole host of people out there today, like the "Nones" (nonreligious)[36] who are turning their backs on all religious institutions and authorities. America is definitely changing in its religious landscape. It is growing ever more secular for a reason.[37] Many have found fault with the church on earth and blame it for a great deal of the ills we experience in this life. The LGBT community is one group among many to lay a lot of blame on the visible church. Just look at the church we see and how it is all over the map on the issue of homosexuality. How has that helped anyone? It's not hard to see why gay people would look at Christians like you and me as a nuisance and as oppressors of their cause. In laying blame on the visible church, I suppose I'm just joining the crowd, and for good reason.

Even as a member and leader in the visible church, I can honestly see why people have a strong dislike or hatred for Christians in general. Admittedly, there were the crusades, which were wars started by the visible church against people of other faiths. If we thought the crusades were bad, how much more was the Spanish Inquisition,[38] which maintained a tradition of executing witches and heretics alike, among other despicable practices.

---

[36] http://www.huffingtonpost.com/gary-laderman/the-rise-of-religious-non_b_2913000.html

[37] Some might argue with the idea that we're becoming more secular. Many who claim to be nonreligious still claim to be spiritual. In such cases, we ought to broaden our view of the definition of religion and "church." For many people today, Facebook has become the old fellowship hall where people can meet, share with each other, and oppose one another. Many preachers and prophets come from Hollywood or Washington DC, carrying no theological degrees but preaching anyway. Scripture lessons come from books, newspapers, and magazines, or the headlines on the web. Sermons are delivered through talk radio, theaters, and TVs alike. Pop music provides the hymns and spiritual songs to underscore what's relevant for people who need to experience something and express themselves in some way. In the end, everybody has religion. The Bible for today seems to be one's own personal self, and as many as there are people, so there seem to be "John 3:16" salvation passages and "gospel" messages.

[38] The Spanish Inquisition (Christian Inquisition) was a movement in the visible church of AD 1400–1800s, which sought to preserve orthodoxy through extreme measures (torture and death), if need be, for perceived reprobates.

The visible church also has a history of denying scientific or undeniable observational fact, such as the heliocentric theory of which Copernicus was a major proponent. And what about the modern-day scandals of TV evangelists or child molestation problems, which the visible church, seemingly, has tried to minimize and cover up almost every step of the way? Members of the LGBT community note things like this often, so let's just come out with it and admit it. The visible church has been a major part of the problem throughout human history.

Truly, the church on earth and its problems are nothing new. It's been like that since Jesus' day. It goes back further still (Exodus 32). The church we see has always been full of wayward clergy and hypocritical laity (Matthew 7:15, 21).

In fact, the visible church on earth was responsible for killing Jesus. It was the religious leaders of Jesus' day who saw to it that he should be crucified. In support of the plot to do away with Jesus, Caiaphas, the high priest at the time, said, "It is better for you that one man should die for the people, not that the whole nation should perish" (John 11:50). One of Jesus' own followers, Judas, betrayed him with a kiss and turned him over to the authorities of the visible church.

This is the very reason that the Scriptures themselves warn against the false people who are within the church on earth—and who often run it. The Bible has described those false people as "wolves in sheep's clothing" (Matthew 7:15) and a "lamb with a dragon's voice" (Revelation 13:11). I can truly understand the bumper sticker that reads: "I don't have a problem with God. It's his followers I can't stand."

At the same time that we lay blame on the visible church for her atrocities, we should encourage people to continue to think through this issue. How could Jesus be good—and all of his followers only evil? Though there may be bitterness toward the church on earth from the LGBT community, many gay people do want to follow Christ and be a part of his holy Christian church. Isn't this why so many of them quote the Scriptures in various ways to try to justify who they are and what they do? We should appreciate the desire expressed by many in the gay community when it comes to Jesus and what he has to say. At the same time, we would do well to point out that it is unfair to blame everyone in the visible church for all the earthly church's failings, and especially for the oppression gay people feel. Certainly there are some good people in the church we see: people who care about God, care about what he thinks, and care for others—especially the poor and oppressed. There are many in the visible church who care about the gay community. Some care so much that they would even be willing to risk speaking the truth in love in a book about homosexuality.

Would it be fair for us to give up on the institution of the visible church on earth because of its faults? Hasn't it served some good somewhere along the line? Could it happen that in throwing out the bathwater, we are in danger of throwing out the baby? Though the church on earth may be to blame for many things, it is not to blame for everything that's wrong in the world. It has also undeniably accomplished much good.[39]

Though the visible church was even guilty of killing Jesus, God's Son, it's not the institution that's at fault. Like anything else, it's always what people do with the institution that makes it good or bad—and sometimes both at the same time. Just as there were some people in the earthly church looking to end Jesus' life, there were also those within the visible church who wanted nothing to do with his condemnation (Luke 23:50–53). They were part of the holy Christian church, the true church, the invisible church.

In the end, Jesus never gave up on the visible church. Not only was it the first place Jesus turned to as he started out his life and ministry (Luke 2:21–32; John 2:13–22), but it was the place he kept coming back to throughout his life and ministry (Luke 4:16). It was

---

[39] The most charitable people are religious people—in particular, those Christians in the "Bible belt" who, in the spirit of New Testament freedom are asked to give freely: http://www.dailyfinance.com/2013/01/22/charitable-giving-most-generous-states/

even the last place he sought before his death (Matthew 21–26). Jesus was always looking to reform the earthly church, to abolish all that was evil, and to restore all that was good (Ephesians 5:25–27).[40] Jesus' ultimate hope was, and still is, that out of the visible church, people will learn of him and become his true church (John 4:23). It's because of this hope of the holy Christian church, among other things, that I remain a part of the visible church.

Nevertheless, on behalf of the visible church, which we can all blame for many things, we can offer sincere apologies to the LGBT community for whatever wrongs they've experienced at the hand of the false church. Wherever true wrongs have been done to that community or to anyone else, those responsible should be held accountable to the fullest extent of the law. God will be their judge. May God be merciful to all of us who are guilty of any wrongdoing, and may he cover us in his grace in Christ before the end of all things!

We should all be aware of this: there's a constant evil within the visible church, one that God's true people are fighting, the same as Jesus did. A book like this is not only a call to the world to give hope on the issue at hand, but it's a calling out to the earthly church to rid itself of many things that are wrong there. We who belong to the true church of God need to feel free to come out about the flaws of the visible church for the sake of others.

The Wicked Witch of the Right and the Left and in Between

There's a saying that you should never talk about religion or politics in mixed company. I guess we're just going to have to smash that rule to smithereens. It's a glaring inconvenience in the blame game we've already begun and have yet to finish. That being the case, I'd like to blame the government next for some of our problems and for many of the problems gay people face.

---

[40] Martin Luther and many of the German Reformers of the 1500s looked to do the same: to clean up the corruption in the Roman Catholic Church of his day.

Perhaps you might expect me to go on and talk about how awful it is that the government is now championing gay rights, which is no real help to gay people. Although the government's action in this regard does deeply sadden me, that's not the flaw I'm looking to point out in this section. Perhaps you're curious to see if I'm going to slam one political party over another. Though any party may have its share of shortcomings, it's not my intent to pick on any parties.

Perhaps you're wondering if I'll point out that this country is in moral decline and that this is a serious situation. As true as that may seem at times, I don't plan on speaking to that here. What I intend to focus on in particular is something I think will surprise you, but it's something that needs to be said, both for the sake of the Christian and for the LGBT community.

Undoubtedly, there's no shortage of blame for the government. In fact, it very often targets itself by laying blame on various political parties, figures, or issues within. Republicans go after Democrats. Democrats get back at Republicans. Liberals can't stand conservatives, and conservatives have no time for liberals. We're divided on foreign policies and domestic issues alike. One person blames the present administration for this, and another blames the previous administration for that.

People blame government and the representatives of government all the time. If you need more proof—which I doubt—just watch any cable news network, listen to some talk radio, or sort through the e-mails, forwards, and blogs in your inbox or on your favorite social network. There's no questioning the fact that those in our government and in our political system are to blame for many problems we face in this life; at least that's what everybody's been saying.

My issue, however, is this: where is the Christian in all of this divisiveness? Sadly, the Christian appears to be found in the thick of things, arguing with the rest of the world as if Christians were no different from anyone else.

Beloved of the Lord, we as a Christian people need to be very careful if we're thinking about blaming those in government—political leaders, whole parties, or anyone on the other side of whatever issue. Many times, going after others can only hurt our witness for Christ and our cause for the gospel.

Did you know that many in the LGBT community have put their hope in the government to deliver them from what they consider to be oppressive Christians? If we Christians choose to lay blame on government or to become uncivil to those with whom we disagree politically by slamming one party over another, what will we accomplish? How will that not cause division among Christians who, by the way, are spread all across the political spectrum? Surely this will divide Christians from the gay people we need to reach.

What will we gain by criticizing a party for one noncritical issue, especially if that party happens to also champion gay rights? What do we gain if we attack a party for generally being for gay rights? We gain nothing. We only lose. We will inadvertently lose a chance to share the gospel with members of the LGBT community.

Paul's words from 1 Corinthians 13:1 come to mind: "If I speak in the tongues of men and of angels, but have not love, I am a noisy gong or a clanging cymbal." God forbid that we would give the impression that our Christian faith is merely a political platform to oppress others who aren't like us. If that's all Christianity boils down to, what good is it? But we Christians know that Christianity has nothing to do with politics.

Besides, what are we hoping to accomplish as Christians if we become determined to use the government to change people's outward behavior? This won't save one soul. And what good would come by Christians blurring the line between their personal political views and the true historic Christian faith? This will only cause someone of one political view to literally "lord" it over someone of another. No souls will be saved that way either. To suggest that one political party is more "Christian" than another is not only false, but it is not helpful to the gospel cause. Even to demand that our country return to a heritage of Christianity—as good as that may sound—will not win people to Christ. It actually might end up driving people further away into self-righteousness or hatred or despair. To me, such an approach toward government is an attempt at making the government into something it's not, something like a savior for society. This should not be, and therein is my complaint.

The apostle John warned believers about the possibility that some would look to the government to save them from all sorts of things, and he prophesied that many would turn to government as if it were God himself (Revelation 13:8). This is why the psalmist wrote, long before John was born, "Put not your trust in princes, in a son of man, in whom there is no salvation" (Psalm 146:3). It was for this form of idolatry (worshipping anything in place of God) that King Nebuchadnezzar lost his empire of Babylon so long ago (Daniel 4:30–37). He demanded that the people see him as divine, as a kind of god and savior—a problem that can tempt Christians in our day as surely as it tempts everyone else.

In order to balance our discussion here, let's consider for a moment the evil of government and its place in the Lord's divine purposes for it. To help us, let's think back to Jesus' day. Not surprising, the government was flawed in the days of Christ. The Roman government was full of leaders who claimed to be gods and to have greater authority than Jesus. It was a government that ultimately sentenced Jesus to be crucified, even though the Roman governor knew Jesus was an innocent man (Luke 23:13–15). It's for reasons like this that the Bible also warns about perpetual corruption in government.

This is not to say that the government was, is, and always will be evil. Whether government is actually serving a holy purpose or an evil one depends on what people do with it. This institution, which God himself put in place, is meant to be a blessing for earthly purposes. An example of this blessing is in the way the early Christians capitalized on the peace of the Romans (*Pax Romana*). In apostolic times, Christians used the stability of the empire and the ease of travel to spread the gospel to the known ends of the earth. In another place, the apostle Paul utilized his Roman citizenship for the preservation of his gospel ministry (Acts 25:11).

Since the government has its place, like the visible church, we aren't to give up on the government. Jesus acknowledged and respected the authority of his governor, even as Jesus was sentenced to death by him (John 19:11). Jesus admired a Roman centurion—a serviceman in a government that opposed the Jews—for his faith, which was greater than any he found among his own people. The man's political allegiance was apparently not an issue for Jesus. Jesus saw how this man could love and serve God even as a Roman (Luke 7:1–10).

In yet another situation, Jesus commanded his followers to give to the government whatever belonged to the government (Matthew 22:21). Jesus' command not only included taxes, but it called for submission, respect, and honor for the government and those who serve, no matter their political affiliations (Romans 13:1, 5–7). It's not that Christians can't have political goals or look to uphold morality in our land for the sake of peace and stability, for this is good (1 Timothy 2:3–4), and there will be many occasions for it. It's just that this can also get in the way of Christ, if we do not approach politics with all gentleness and respect and with gospel intent.

Admittedly, it is no easy task for the Christian to live in two kingdoms: the true church and the civil government. We can see the difficult situation we're in now because of how Christians have approached politics at times. When Christians speak on homosexuality today, it automatically makes people believe they're just being political. Nevertheless, it is essential that we do the kingdom work through the invisible church and live peaceful, upright lives in the world, making the most of all opportunities to attract everyone to the holy Christian church and to Christ.

Wherever we fail at this and abuse the government by blurring the line between politics and faith, we need to do the honest thing and admit our wrongs. In reflecting on the flaws of the government and in confessing that we Christians contribute to the problem at times, we may win people over to the real Savior, even those who tragically look to the government as a kind of savior. If Christians can rise above the pitfalls of politics, it can only help our witness of Christ to the LGBT community.

The Wicked Witch of Higher Learning

Moving on down the line of blame, I think we might as well stop in and visit our institutions of higher learning, including and especially many seminaries. These are the places we often look to for solutions to all our problems, so it seems a natural place for us to lay a little blame. After all, we still have lots of problems, whether we're talking about homosexuality and the hard lives gay people live or other issues facing humanity. Of course, gay people may think they have a friend in the Wicked Witch of Higher Learning, because, in general, these institutions support their lifestyle. But are the institutions of higher learning really anybody's friend on this matter?

Philosophy is a word that comes to mind when I think of higher learning. Philosophy is the discipline that systematically evaluates our existence as humans and seeks to address our universal problems in the hope of leading us to a better way of life. Right now, we might be thinking about ancient philosophers such as Socrates, Plato, and Aristotle. We generally recognize these figures to be the pioneers in the field of philosophy, among other things—at least for the western world.

After them, we may think of a whole host of people who, through the ages, added to the subject of philosophy. They are too many to name. If you have no one in mind, that's okay. As lofty as philosophy tends to be, it seems at times—dare I say it?—impractical. But it is a force to be reckoned with, for it has much more power over us than we might think.

Today, it is critical for us to know that the dominant philosophical trend of our western culture is postmodernism. Even more critical is to know what that means and how it's impacting us in our thinking. Suffice it to say that postmodernism is a seedbed for homosexuality to flourish, among many other things. If you are unfamiliar with postmodernism, allow me to define it as simply as I can. (My hope in this oversimplification is to save us from needing to pop a couple of aspirin at the end of this section because of brain overload. You should know that defining postmodernism is no easy feat, especially since some people suggest that we have yet to reach the end of its development.)[41]

In short, postmodernism holds that concepts like truth, morality, and even reality are all relative or relational to individuals. In other words, these concepts aren't universally fixed as practically all philosophies of the past assumed. Postmodernism says that truth, morality, and reality are things we look to construct in different ways, depending on the interaction of people and people groups. We might need some aspirin after all.

Let me illustrate what I'm saying with a few philosophical worldviews that led up to the present view of postmodernism. Let's say that you have an apple in your hand. One religious philosophical worldview says, "That is an apple. God made it so. It's undeniable because the Scriptures say he made it 'according to its kind.' Even if my senses and observation should deny it, what you have is an apple."[42] Another philosopher comes along with his worldview and says, "This is indeed an apple. However, since God cannot be observed, I conclude this is an apple by what I observe with my senses and deduce by my human reason. Logically, then, not only is this an apple, but here is proof of God. This apple had to come

---

[41] "That postmodernism is indefinable is a truism. However, it can be described as a set of critical, strategic and rhetorical practices employing concepts such as difference, repetition, the trace, the simulacrum, and hyperreality to destabilize other concepts such as presence, identity, historical progress, epistemic certainty, and the univocity of meaning" (Gary Aylesworth, "Postmodernism," *The Stanford Encyclopedia of Philosophy*, ed. Edward N. Zalta, Summer 2013 edition, forthcoming URL = <http://plato.stanford.edu/archives/sum2013/entries/postmodernism/>.

[42] Reformation of the Church (AD 1500–1600s). For centuries in the West, before the time of the Reformation, "the truth" was purported to be whatever the Roman Catholic Church called it.

from somewhere, and God is the first cause. It just so happens that the Scripture is true in this regard."[43] Another philosopher comes along and says, "This is indeed an apple. Truly, our senses confirm that, and our human reason affirms it. As for God, who knows if he exists? The apple could have come about by natural means, which is just as reasonable to conclude. And not just the apple, but the Bible must have also come about by natural means. God is inconsequential to our discussion."[44]

Finally, postmodernism says, "This may very well be an apple as you perceive it, whether by your senses, your human reason, or your holy book. At least, it is an apple to you. However, others might say it's an orange, and they might have good reason for that, as they perceive it and use their reason or interpret their holy books. If there were more of them than you, and if they had power on their side, history would report that this is an orange and not an apple. In a hundred years, who knows what we'll call things like this? So, can we know with all certainty that this is an apple? If it is an apple, then it's not because truth says so or reality demands it to be—as if those concepts exist in an absolute sense. It's an apple simply because that's what a number of people agreed upon. The same is true when it comes to God or the Bible.

"What makes one or the other a 'truth' and a 'kind of reality' and even things with 'moral' implications are people groups. The more important question we should be asking is, what's their agenda? Why do people define the apple as they do? Reason might suggest that you are only concluding that this is an apple to marginalize a minority group who feel like it's really an orange. Why can't it be something else to them? The same goes for God and the Bible.

"Who is to say that your truth is reality and that your morality is truth? Why can't another group's truth be true, real, and moral? Isn't this issue of the apple more of a power struggle than anything

---

[43] Enlightenment or Age of Reason/Rationalism (AD 1600–1700s).

[44] Modernism (AD 1800–1900s) includes naturalism, Darwinism, secular humanism, theistic existentialism, etc.

else? Honestly, can we possibly know with all certainty what this 'apple' is, or if it is even anything at all? As to that, what is 'is' anyway? Doesn't the concept of an apple simply depend on what different people groups make of it in the histories they write for their own purposes? Doesn't this matter entirely depend on the language they use, defined according to their beliefs and what they choose to impose on the oppressed?"

Granted, it may seem a little comical to go on about an apple like this, but I think the philosophy of postmodernism is more easily understood by it. Perhaps we can better understand the implications of this philosophy if we replace the word *apple* with whatever issues are at hand—like the issue of homosexuality.

In regard to the postmodern view presented in this illustration, replace the word *apple* with a moral view that was once generally accepted. This should explain why many of those same views are now up for debate today. This may also explain how people can live lives that seem to conflict in thought, word, and action. There are those who may suffer no pangs of conscience when they join one organization while speaking or living contrary to its basic tenets among another people group. This may be why some people join multiple organizations, all of which are fundamentally opposed to all the others. If a person constructs his own truth, why can't he exchange truths at will, depending on where he is or whom he's with?

With postmodernism, boundaries become superficial. Authorities are unsubstantiated. Meaning becomes universally meaningless. Tolerance is the only thing that can be championed.[45] Tragically, nothing is truly certain. This includes Jesus and his cross. They too

---

[45] The virtue of tolerance seems to be the prevailing principle to live by in our day. It permeates the visible church at large, the government, and an increasing number of individuals. Yet, what is seen as "tolerance" today is actually a cloak for acceptance. Many people demand that others embrace or accept their views as equal rather than tolerate them. To tolerate, by definition, means to disagree with but to put up with out of love. Tolerance is not acceptance. It is actually the opposite.

are reduced to mere crutches for people in this life. Jesus, Christianity, and his Word are viewed as attempts to gain power over others.

Following in the footsteps of Nietzsche, one of the fathers of postmodernism, we hear this new philosophy proclaim, "God is dead." As a consequence, all absolute meaning is dead too.[46] For postmodernists, this leveling of all worldviews isn't meant to be bad. In its nature, this philosophy looks to make all viewpoints equal. Like Robin Hood, it takes the power away from the strong and gives it to the oppressed.

But in the end, figuratively speaking, how does this philosophy not crucify Christ all over again? At the same time, how is this philosophy not fundamentally flawed? On the one hand, it claims that all ideas are equal. On the other hand, by that very claim, it denies the possibility of absolutism, which speaks out against relativism.

Postmodernism strikes at all the previous foundations that society has been built upon, philosophies that previously provided some order and stability to our society. Tragically, postmodernism may not leave much of a foundation in their places. To use a biblical illustration, postmodernism wrecks the "tower of Babel" of philosophies, past and present, and looks to build its own monument out of the rubble. It has yet to be seen whether or not the material it uses for building can hold a society together. Due to its nature, it's an inevitable certainty that this philosophy will merely further fragment our society, as it can only pit one group against another (Genesis 11:1–9).

To sum up, postmodernism is a natural curse from God, which he has allowed as the consequence of humanity's arrogance in denying

---

[46] Nihilism (nothingness or meaninglessness) was what Nietzsche recognized as the inevitable consequence of "killing God." Concepts that are denied by this philosophy are truth, morality, and the reality of absolutes. Though Nietzsche called nihilism the "crisis of humanity," he hoped that one day humanity would find a way to rise above it and find meaning anyway. Interestingly enough, King Solomon concluded that nihilism was the only inevitability, after he took a look at life apart from God, a life "under the sun." He proclaimed about an existence without God, "Vanity of vanities" (Ecclesiastes 1:2). In the end, Solomon found no solution for the problem of nihilism, except to return to and trust in the Lord.

him and his Word as the only source of truth. Whatever the future holds for this philosophy, it would seem that we have simply returned to an ancient form of skepticism that ends up bringing chaos to all creation as it sets in motion the perpetual question: "Did God really say?" (Genesis 3:1).

Due to the consequences of this present philosophy, which is more of a wrecking ball than anything else, it's only fitting to lay blame at the doorstep of "higher learning." This philosophy grants permission for anyone in society to believe that homosexuality is okay, and this way of thinking is influencing our own people and especially our youth, whether they are gay or straight.

I'm not intending to say that institutions of higher learning are in and of themselves corrupt. Gaining wisdom is something the Scriptures call us to do as a matter of utmost importance. The Bible says that gaining wisdom is a matter of life and death (Proverbs 9). However, if the pursuit of wisdom leads us to false wisdom (Proverbs 1:7), then it can't amount to any eternal good. In these last days, because of the corruption of higher learning, the Bible is constantly calling out, "Where is the one who is wise?" (1 Corinthians 1:19–20, 25). I think it's appropriate for us to be asking today, "How much godly wisdom is being offered through higher learning in light of postmodernism's overwhelming influence?"[47] It is essential for us to recognize that there is one absolute truth.

Where this knowledge of postmodernism becomes terribly practical for a typical congregation like ours is in seeing the walls of unbelief we are up against. In regard to homosexuality, we will only find more of a hardening of the heart because of this philosophy. As we look to live in the world, we need to know that many people give a pass to both the government and institutions of higher learning, especially concerning truth and authority. Rarely, if ever, will people critique

---

[47] A great and quick read to better understand various worldviews like postmodernism, which we all will encounter, is the book by author David C. Thompson entitled, *What in the World Is Going On?* You can find it at www.nph.net (Northwestern Publishing House).

these institutions—at least not the segments they are part of. We have a difficult job before us as the holy Christian church in reaching people.

The Wicked Witch Within

The list could go on and on about who's guilty of oppressing gay people, either by condemning them for their lifestyle or by giving them permission to embrace it. How about corporate America, which funds the LGBT cause regularly in their support of gay initiatives or pride parades? What about the media and all its spin, or Hollywood and all its glitter and influence without substance? How about all the adults out there who avoid responsibility whenever possible and support this issue or remain silent on it so as not to offend? What about parents who fail to discipline their own children or bring them up in the Lord regarding homosexuality? How about kids who rebel against authority, following the influence of their peers as they champion and fight for what is perverse? How about all those who are judgmental over this issue? What about ... (fill in the human blank)? Surely all of these entities have had a hand in hurting gay people in one way or another. No wonder gay people feel oppressed. No wonder we all do in some way.

How about me? Am I to blame at all? (If only we had stopped playing the blame game a little earlier! But you can't go changing the rules in the middle of the game.) Okay, so I admit it. I too am to blame. To the core, I'm selfish. I'm a regular Dr. Jekyll and Mr. Hyde. I'm a hypocrite more times than I'd care to admit. I don't always practice what I preach, and this speaks to my deepest regret. It's not that I want to be this way; I just can't help it (Romans 7:14–25). That's not intended to be an excuse. I'm willing to own up to all I am and all I do. I will even admit that I should be damned eternally for all that I am in my nature. I think it would be good for gay people to know this about me too. I am guilty of remaining silent about homosexuality in certain instances. I have also been guilty of being too harsh in speaking on the issue.

As to blaming me, I'll even dare to say that I'm solely responsible for the death of Jesus. That is to say, if I were the only sinner in the world—and I am a sinner—he would have been put to death for me alone. I have loved myself more than my neighbors, and therefore I have loved myself more than God. Surely all my damnable faults were more than enough to nail Jesus to a tree. Because of that, I'll admit that I'm as responsible as anybody for the mess we're in (1 Timothy 1:15). In the end, I'm part of the flawed church and part of an imperfect government, and every day I see that I often live by my own sinful nature's philosophy.

I can only blame myself for all the problems I see among the human race. It's all caused by people who are just like me by nature. This is why I have lost my faith in humanity. How can I put my faith in anyone else? I can't even completely trust myself. I'm often without a heart, without reason, and without the courage to do what I should. At times, I'm completely lost in this surreal world. The sins in my own life are all the proof I need.

As I look at myself—as I examine my thoughts, words, and actions—I know why everything is so terribly messed up. Humanity is much more the problem than it is the solution for anything. We are the common thread running throughout all that's wrong. It's our sin within that's given way to all our struggles. Isn't that what the blame game has shown us in the end?[48] Is there anybody truly blameless?

The Wizard of Oz

What about God? I suppose many might demand that we lay some blame on him too. Gay people, as oppressed as they are, are bombarded with temptations to blame God, especially in those moments when they can't understand why they're gay. Who of us can't relate in some way and understand where they're coming from? Who of us hasn't

---

[48] So much for humanism!

accused God of wrongdoing as we face our own personal issues and hardships in life?

Whenever any of us are tempted to believe that God might be to blame for any hardship we face, we might want to take a page out of postmodernism: Can we be absolutely sure about that? Or let's consider the reasoning that atheists must employ. To atheists, he's not even real. They suggest that people made him up, similar to what a fictitious circus magician did in creating the Wizard of Oz when he entered into the Land of Oz. That man duped everybody into believing that he was a grand wizard capable of solving all their problems. He then went on to bolster his claim through some pyrotechnics, a projection screen, and some surround sound, all behind a cheap curtain. He was just a fraud. That's what atheists claim about God too. The whole concept of God is just a fraud to them.

But how can anyone blame God if, by chance, he doesn't exist? Atheists may be on to something in this regard. Before anybody else, they may be the first to say that we can't blame God for the evil we see. Of course, if there's nobody but us humans to blame, then we must undoubtedly take all the blame ourselves.

For those who are unsure about God (agnostics), there may be a strong inclination to blame God, if he does exist. We can also understand where agnostics are coming from. Who hasn't blamed God at times when hearing about a tragedy? We return to all the questions of our opening: Why are there tsunamis? Why are there earthquakes? Why are there asteroids and plagues? Why is humanity so corrupt in so many ways? Why do gay people have it so hard, among so many others? How is God *not* somehow to blame, if everything came from him?

Those questions give way to many more: If God does exist, why doesn't he fix all our problems? Does he not fix them because he is an angry God who is only looking to destroy us—like Dorothy first believed about the Wizard of Oz? Could God really be helpless, like the fumbling buffoon that the Wizard of Oz turned out to be in the end? If God is angry with us or helpless to save us—if he is to blame

Rainbow Savior

in any way—then the best we can hope for is that this is all just a bad dream. If we can't save ourselves—which history proves is the case—and if God can't save us, what hope is there? I'd suggest that if there is no God, or if God is to blame in any way, we are all lost, and there's no point in carrying on. Who else can fix the mess we're in?

But what if there is a God, and what if he's absolutely good? (Psalm 14:1; Mark 10:18). Suppose the heavens declare his glory and the heavens prove the work of his hands (Psalm 19:1). What if God is without blame? (Psalm 18:30). Not only that, but couldn't there be a possibility that God is able to rescue us all on his own? (Isaiah 43:11). Suppose he has plans for you, plans not to harm you but to prosper you, to give you a hope and a future in Christ (Jeremiah 29:11). And what if, in Christ, God has already provided a solution for all our problems, one that will be made clear in the end? (Ephesians 1:9–10).

Someone might say that there are a lot of *ifs* here about God. Still, that doesn't mean that these ifs rule out all possibility. In the end, I'd suggest that this is the only hope left to the human race. It's the only hope we've ever had, as surely as the psalmist wrote, "I lift up my eyes to the hills. From where does my help come? My help comes from the LORD, who made heaven and earth" (Psalm 121:1).

We have tried to fix the mess we're in for thousands of years now, but, admittedly, we have been miserably unsuccessful. I'll even argue that things are only getting worse. What people have been able to end the oppression felt by gay people—or anyone else for that matter? Will people ever be able to fix things on their own? Absolutely not. God must save us, and God must do this alone. Is it possible that the human race has been getting in the way of this from the time we fell into sin? The Bible proclaims as much (Ecclesiastes 7:29).

What if there is a God who loves us unconditionally? (Romans 5:8). Some believe that every good thing we have is from him (James 1:17). What if he is the reason the sun rises and the rain falls and provides nourishment for both the righteous and wicked alike? (Matthew 5:45). Not only that, but there are those who know that he is not some impersonal force but is personally near to each and every one of us (Acts 17:27). What if we live and move and have our being in him, and what if we are all his children? (Acts 17:28). Surely the psalmist had it right in Psalm 139:1–18a.

> O Lord, you have searched me and known me! You know when I sit down and when I rise up; you discern my thoughts from afar. You search out my path and my lying down and are acquainted with all my ways. Even before a word is on my tongue, behold, O Lord, you know it altogether. You hem me in, behind and before, and lay your hand upon me. Such knowledge is too wonderful for me; it is high; I cannot attain it. Where shall I go from your Spirit? Or where shall I flee from your presence? If I ascend to heaven, you are there! If I make my bed in Sheol [the abode of the dead], you are there! If I take the wings of the morning and dwell in the uttermost parts of the sea, even there your hand shall lead me, and your right hand shall hold me. If I say, "Surely the darkness shall cover me, and the light about me be night, even the darkness is not dark to you; the night is bright as the day, for darkness is as light with you. For you formed my inward parts; you knitted me together in my mother's womb. I praise you, for I am fearfully and wonderfully made. Wonderful are your works; my soul knows it very well. My frame was not hidden from you, when I was being made in secret, intricately woven in the depths of the earth. Your eyes saw my unformed substance; in your book were written, every one of them, the days that were formed for me, when as yet there was none of them. How precious to me are your thoughts, O God! How vast is the sum of them! If I would count them, they are more than the sand. (Psalm 139:1–18a)

What if everything evil we suffer along with all our hardships is in spite of God? (Genesis 3:2–3). Suppose all of our struggles and our misunderstanding about God are not by his design. What if other influences—whether from within us or from outside us and apart from God—are to blame? (Genesis 3:6; John 1:4–5, 9–10). What if something evil has been trying to keep everyone from him all along? (Revelation 12:9).

Nevertheless, is it possible that he has been communicating to us this entire time in a still, small voice so as to comfort and not to frighten us? (Exodus 20:19; 1 Kings 19:11–13). At the same time, it's possible that God remains hidden behind a veil, because anyone imperfect who sees him can only die (Exodus 33:20). What if he has the answer to all our problems and has given us time to think on all these things so that one day we may see him and live? (2 Peter 3:9). The Christian knows that God alone can make sense out of our lives and give us the answers to all our questions and problems (1 Corinthians 13:12). This is a part of the reason why God handed Jesus over to die for us all (Acts 17:30–31).

The Narrow Road: The Way Back Home

Beloved of the Lord, see how our God and his Word are the only answers for our problems! We understand this Scriptural reasoning here about God and us, and we have the privilege to share it with a community and world that's desperate for it. Let's continue on our journey now to understand what is going on in the churches at large, in our society, and with the institution of marriage, so that we might be kept from any great spiritual harm and so that we might free others from all oppression.

In our study of many of the issues we face with homosexuality in our society, may the Lord keep pointing us back to the narrow road of faith in Christ, the way back home for all of us through the Scriptures! May we come to the destination the Rainbow Savior desires to lead all his people to, and may we bring many from the LGBT community and the world with us!

10

The Church for LGBTs

Whenever I drive east to head into Minneapolis, I pass by a church with a rainbow banner for all to see. There are countless others like it, no doubt. Do you know what the church there is saying by that? That church wants all people to know that LGBTs are welcome there. They especially want members of the LGBT community to know that they can find a home with them. These are the churches that boast about themselves, "All are welcome!"

Churches like that stand in stark contrast to another church in Topeka, Kansas, known as the Westboro Baptist Church. At Westboro you will find no rainbow flags. The last time I checked, you'll only find a banner that says, "God hates America." Wherever they gather, you'll often find picket signs in the same vein, damning gays especially. Very few people are welcome in this congregation of about forty members.

The media gives the impression that these are the only two kinds of churches out there when it comes to homosexual people. Churches either welcome gays and embrace them as they are, or they hate them and hope they burn in hell. Surely those aren't the only kinds of churches out there!

Do the churches that say "All are welcome!" really welcome LGBTs and everyone? Are all the other churches only showing hatred toward gay people? What kind of congregation are we? Most important, what can help us distinguish the churches of God from those that aren't?

For the sake of our congregation and for all those in the LGBT community, we'll look to address the issue of the visible Christian church at large and why there is such a division among churches on the topic of homosexuality.

The Radical Churches

Let's begin with the "Westboro" types. It troubles me deeply that there are churches like these which preach condemnation for gay people. I don't understand why they are doing what they do. The Jesus they are proclaiming is not the Jesus of the Bible. Apparently they mistake the holiness of God and his sovereignty as an inability to distinguish a sinner from his sin in a time of grace. As they overemphasize God's righteousness, which eradicates sin, they fail to see that it's in this same righteousness that God delivers the sinner from that sin—even the worst of sinners (1 Timothy 1:15–17).

That passage from 1 Timothy, which speaks of saving the worst of sinners, is a reference to the apostle Paul, whose sin was not immorality but self-righteous zeal and a condemning spirit. In other words, the worst of sinners are often not those entangled in immorality but those ensnared in a holier-than-thou attitude. Members of the Westboro congregation would do well to contemplate Jesus' parable of the two sons, which illustrates that very point (Matthew 21:28–32).

Many homosexuals are actually closer to the kingdom of God than members of Westboro who carry around picket signs stating that God hates gays. Jesus told the Pharisees, who considered themselves faultless in their legalism: "Truly, I say to you, the tax collectors and prostitutes go into the Kingdom of God before you" (Matthew 21:31).

In the failing theology of Westboro, there is an overemphasis of the law of God that overshadows the gospel,[49] the only power to redeem anyone. Instead of saying that certain people are too sick to be saved, Westboro should strive to be like Jesus and reach out to those whom they believe to be especially sin-sick. And before we call the sexually immoral sicker than others, Westboro might want to consider if there is anything sicker than condemning people of the LGBT community, especially those who recognize their sin and are desperate for a way out.

Jesus thinks that people who have no time for sinners are the sickest sinners of them all. For the Pharisees who got angry with Jesus for reaching out to prostitutes and tax collectors, Jesus always had the most condemning of words. He said to them, "Those who are well have no need of a physician, but those who are sick. I came not to call the righteous, but sinners" (Mark 2:17). There truly are no greater words of condemnation than those words that Jesus spoke to the self-righteous. In essence, Jesus was saying that he will abandon all the self-righteous to eternal hell in the hopes of rescuing broken sinners from that same hell.

The Westboro Baptist Church is not a church that God is pleased with, as they, in their self-righteousness, show hatred for others. Jesus still died for every member of Westboro, but he hates what they're doing. No one there who holds to their present theology should consider themselves justified before the Lord. I would hope that such souls in jeopardy of eternal fire would take a moment to read another parable about a Pharisee and a tax collector (Luke 18:9–14). Jesus' most stinging words were not aimed at "sinners" but at the self-righteous who are among the greatest sinners of all (Matthew 23).

---

[49] The Law – All which God demands of us and which only threatens us with eternal death as we fail. The Gospel – All which God has accomplished for us in Christ alone by grace which completely satisfies the demands of the Law and pays the punishment of all its threats.

Rev. William A. Monday

The Rainbow Churches

On August 21, 2009, the Evangelical Lutheran Church of America (ELCA), the largest "Lutheran" church in the world, voted to welcome the LGBT community into their ranks of clergy. For quite a while, they had already welcomed gays into their fellowship and had only banned non-celibate homosexuals from filling their pulpits. On that day, by a vote of 551 to 459 in downtown Minneapolis, the ELCA symbolically hoisted the rainbow flag over their church body,[50] joining a growing number of other mainline denominations whose banners are already raised in flying colors.

Whenever a church does something like this, it is a monumental change. It is also a rare opportunity to see a church's true doctrinal colors. Think for a moment what this means to the world and especially to those who join congregations of these church bodies.

Historically, homosexuality has been understood as a sin. Historically, the visible Christian church at large has declared that people who willingly live in such a way cannot enter into the kingdom of Heaven (1 Corinthians 6:9). Historically, the visible Christian church has been unanimous about this—that is, until these most recent days.

My questions to these church bodies that are now flying the rainbow overhead are these: Has the visible church been wrong on this issue all these years? If so, how many people have wrongfully been condemned through this historic teaching of the Christian church? Have apologies been issued to those victims and their families? Will apologies even do, if the holy church—the true spiritual forefathers of all present Christians—have so burdened consciences unfairly that poor souls had no choice but to despair of life altogether?

If the holy Christian church has been wrong on this and has gathered this teaching from the Scriptures, then what good is the Christian church—or the Scriptures? What else is wrong about the

---

[50] http://www.washingtonpost.com/wp-dyn/content/article/2009/08/21/AR2009082103343.html (ELCA lifts ban on gay clergy, August 2009)

church and the Bible? In a hundred years, will we find that Jesus isn't the only way to heaven as the Bible undeniably claims he is? (John 14:6; Acts 4:12). If one thing is wrong, especially as blatant as this is, how is anything else reliable in the church or the Word of God?

I know some of the answers to these questions. Some will say that the Bible is God's Word but that this doesn't mean it is without error. To that, I say, can't a perfect God make a perfect book through imperfect humans and preserve it perfectly for all time? Nevertheless, many people reason that since it was written by man, it must have errors. God apparently isn't powerful enough to make his Word perfect or to preserve his Word perfectly through imperfect people.

Some churches have bought into a modern idea to deny all that's supernatural in regard to the Word and what it says. In their thinking, they have become free to hold to what they want to, and to disregard the rest when it's expedient. In these last days, many in these churches think it's advantageous to accept homosexuality. They believe that it's the only loving thing to do, so that's what they do.

Some go so far as to say that who Jesus is and what he wants us to know about him isn't fully contained in the Bible anyway. They believe that God continues to give them more appropriate revelations today to better decipher what applies in the Bible and what doesn't. This is why a church body can ban homosexuals from their pulpits at one convention, but at the next one, they can welcome them in.[51] Did you know that such churches can only do so because they distinguish Jesus Christ, the Word made flesh, from all his teachings, the Word in print?[52] That seems logical, but it's not what God has asked the holy Christian church to do. God wants us to see Christ and the written Word as indistinguishable in regard to knowing him in any and every way in this life (1 Corinthians 2:11–16).

---

[51] http://www.jsonline.com/news/religion/29295814.html (2007 ELCA upholds ban on gay clergy); ibid (ELCA lifts ban, August 2009)

[52] This is the case with the ELCA (http://www.wlsessays.net/files/BrugELCA2012.pdf).

In his famous Sermon on the Mount, Jesus taught us not to make any distinction between him and the Scriptures when he said, "Do not think that I have come to abolish the Law or the Prophets; I have not come to abolish them but to fulfill them. For truly, I say to you, until heaven and earth pass away, not an iota, not a dot, will pass from the Law until all is accomplished" (Matthew 5:17–18).

People who think God relays revelations to them outside the Scriptures in these last days will eventually adopt ideas that run contrary to the Scriptures. We need not expect any more revelations since Christ came, and the eye witnesses, prophets, and apostles now only wait to return with him and all the hosts of heaven. What new revelations could still come that would enhance or surpass the greatest revelations already given in the Old and New Testaments concerning Jesus Christ? It seems that the scriptural answer to that is, "There are none" (Hebrews 1:1–2).[53]

After so much human history, the visible church at large has yet to learn that the Devil always tempts us with the very first temptation: "Did God actually say?" (Genesis 3:1). Isn't this one of the reasons why there are so many different denominations and why more and more denominations accept things that contradict the Bible? This universal reasoning, inside and outside the church on earth, of obtaining greater enlightenment anywhere but in the Word of God is a sign that we are nearing the end of all things.

Paul said, "Now the Spirit expressly says that in later times some will depart from the faith by devoting themselves to deceitful spirits and teachings of liars whose consciences are seared" (1 Timothy 4:1–2). In his second letter to Timothy, he went on to say, "For the time is coming when people will not endure sound teaching, but having itching ears they will accumulate for themselves teachers to

---

[53] If the Scriptures by chance were "open" and not "closed" to more revelation toward the end of time, those separate revelations would never contradict what has already been written. They would only further support them. Due to the complete nature of the Scriptures, I personally am not waiting for any new revelations, and I would most certainly be minded to test everything new against the touchstone of God's inspired, inerrant Word.

suit their own passions, and will turn away from listening to the truth and wander off into myths" (2 Timothy 4:3–4).

To further understand that the rainbow churches have added to the Word of God and have thereby subtracted from it—something the Lord himself condemns through the last apostle John (Revelation 22:12–19)—we need to consider the specific error that these churches have fallen into. If the Westboro church has fallen into the error of emphasizing the law of God and its threat at the expense of the gospel of grace, then the ELCA-like churches have emphasized the gospel of grace at the expense of the law of God and its threat. That is to say, the rainbow churches have turned God's grace into a license to sin (Romans 6:1–14).

The rainbow churches are proclaiming to the world that God loves everybody. Never mind what they do, as long as it is generally acceptable to the society in which they live. At least when it comes to the issue of homosexuality, this is what those churches are preaching. Deep down, they know they cannot abandon God's law, but to get around this, they change that law in the name of the gospel of grace. This is why the ELCA in particular has tried to define homosexuality as acceptable—as long as it is "publicly accountable, lifelong, monogamous."[54]

Honestly, isn't this new doctrine born of worldly pressure? Isn't this false view also born of a false understanding of the Bible? Under the principle of love, as they define it, they believe they can alter God's written Word in any way that seems right to them. It is not the true church's role or attitude—or even a possibility—to change the mind of Christ. It is the holy Christian church's role and attitude only to submit to Christ's mind in all things (Ephesians 5:24a).

To soothe their troubled consciences, the rainbow churches reason that Christ, the real Word, wants them to show love, which in our day must now be defined as always accepting both the sinner and all behavior that society deems acceptable. This is how they can accept

---

[54] http://www.elca.org/News-and-Events/6587

something that the Bible clearly calls a sin. To further ease their troubled consciences, they lump this issue, among other things, into the category of Christian freedom (disputable matters).[55] They teach that we should never bind anyone's conscience on a matter like this, whether one is for homosexuality or against it.

They have become skilled in misapplying Romans 14:1–4, which speaks of things God has neither commanded nor forbidden. Homosexuality and all sexual immorality do not fall under disputable matters.[56] This explains why some churches in the same church body can refuse to accept gay clergy, while others embrace them without a word from the leaders of their denomination. All of this is nothing less than preaching the gospel without a need for it. It is the gospel at the expense of the law, which is no gospel at all (Galatians 1:8).

At the end of the day, it is as unloving for any church to say that God loves you and accepts your sin as it is to say that God hates you because of your sin. We are not called to be "holier-than-thou," but we are also not called to accept anything that God clearly condemns in the Scriptures. Furthermore, neither of these two kinds of churches would be able to welcome all people. The radical churches will not welcome certain kinds of sinners, while the rainbow churches won't welcome those who preach against certain kinds of sin. I am positive that I would never be welcome to preach the message of this book in a pulpit of a rainbow church, while someone with the opposite message would be more than welcome.

Just as I pray for Westboro and all the radical churches, I pray that the rainbow churches would learn to be bold in accepting all of God's Word and to put off the worldly thinking that they have fallen victim to. In particular, I do not look to condemn the ELCA, but I simply speak to the falsehood that is there in the hopes that those guilty of it will turn away from that falsehood for the sake of souls.

---

[55] These are things that God neither commands nor forbids in the Holy Scriptures, and therefore Christians are free to do them or not to do them. Disputable matters are also called *adiaphora* (*mitteldinge*).

[56] Ibid., (bound conscience).

Rainbow Savior

I pray that there can be reform among all the rainbow churches as they realize that demonstrating true love means to be faithful to all of God's Word. That is what is best for souls.

The preachers who serve in such congregations should know too that they will be called to give an account for their teaching, and as supposed teachers of God's Word, they will be judged more harshly (James 3:1). Those who have been given a trust must prove faithful (1 Corinthians 4:2). Otherwise, they will be condemned or, at best, will only escape as ministers passing through the flames (1 Corinthians 3:10–15).

The message of this chapter goes out to those leaders in all mainline churches under the rainbow banner. All the rainbow churches have fallen into the trap of sinful reasoning, which claims that the Word of God isn't entirely reliable anymore for our times. Only when such leaders and their churches return to all the truths of Scripture will they be churches that can welcome all. If there is to be any reform in these churches, my guess is that it will have to come from the laity.

The Repentance Churches

If the radical churches are not the ones who welcome all, and if the rainbow churches are not the ones who welcome all, then are there any churches that truly welcome anyone and everyone? There are. By the grace of God, there are many churches that truly welcome all. The churches that are faithful to the Scriptures in their entirety truly welcome anyone and everyone.

The churches that are truly for LGBTs are those that preach the full message of repentance. Repentance is defined as turning away from one's sin and having faith to believe that Jesus saved us from that sin. The churches that preach repentance concerning all sin—no matter how popular or unpopular—are those who ensure that the message of the law and its threat serves the greater message of the gospel of grace. These are the churches that Paul would say are "rightly handling the word of truth" (2 Timothy 2:15). They are the churches that "preach the word ... ready in season and out of season; [which] reprove, rebuke, and exhort with complete patience and teaching ... sober-minded, enduring hardship" as they reach out to win more souls for Christ and to fulfill all the duties of their ministries (2 Timothy 4:1–5). This was the kind of ministry John the Baptist was known for.

The true welcoming churches are not necessarily the popular ones. They rarely are. These churches are not necessarily the bigger ones either. These churches are hardly ever counted among the strong. They indeed often look weak (Revelation 3:7–13). Though looks can be deceiving, there is something offered from these churches for all people. These churches are those that welcome all to repent—no matter who they are, where they're at in life, or where they come from. They welcome all, as they never give up on the impenitent. The impenitent are those who are hardened in their sin, whether they're self-righteous or immoral. These churches welcome all, especially those with penitent hearts. The penitent are those who are sorry for all their sin and who put their faith in Christ to deliver them from their sin.

The repentance churches do not welcome all ideas or messages into their midst, nor any sin—especially not from their pulpits—but they do welcome all people of varying points of view to go to the Scriptures and become one in thought and mind as the Lord wills (Ephesians 4:11–13). The repentance churches are those that hold to the Word of God alone as they suffer with Christ for their faithfulness to the Word. They look just like their Lord in this regard. They are humble and bear all things so that some might be saved, as surely as Jesus suffered on the cross to love all and especially to save those who believe.

The truly welcoming churches follow in the footsteps of all the prophets and apostles. After all, they are built on all the prophets' and apostles' teaching, with Christ as the only cornerstone. When we consider the ways of those saints of old, we can recognize more easily which churches belong to those ways and to Christ as their head.

The writer to the Hebrews characterized the lives of the faithful when he said of their faithfulness to the Word that they are those who "shut the mouths of the lions, quenched the fury of the flames, and escaped the edge of the sword; [they are those] whose weakness was turned to strength ... [they were] tortured, refusing to be released ... [they] faced jeers and flogging, and even chains and imprisonment. They were put to death by stoning; they were sawed in two; they were killed by the sword. They went about in sheepskins and goatskins, destitute, persecuted and mistreated— the world was not worthy of them. They wandered in deserts and mountains, living in caves and in holes in the ground. These were all commended for their faith" (Hebrews 11:33–39), a faith in the entirety of the Word of God.

Do you see the common thread running through the prophets and apostles from God that also runs through his true Christian church? All were faithful to his Word, even when the world put them to suffering and death for it. God's people, his true churches and leaders, are those who are in the world but who do not go along with the world when the world opposes God's will (John 17:14–15). The rainbow churches don't fit this description. It is clear that they are in league with the world in their support of homosexuality. The radical churches don't fit this description either. They are neither in line with the world nor with God's message of grace.

The Recluse Churches

I suppose there's one more kind of church out there that doesn't exactly fit into any of the previous categories. It would be good for us to know about them too, since all faithful congregations will be tempted to go the same way, if we don't follow the ways of the radical and rainbow churches. The other kind of church out there is the silent church, which is sending soft and unclear messages on LGBT issues. I choose to label them the "recluse" churches.

These are the churches that withdraw from speaking on this topic even among their own people. They apparently reason that it's politically divisive and that they wouldn't make much progress on it anyway. There is no cross to bear in being silent on issues as intense as this one, and so, admittedly, this seems to be a pleasing way to go. Can you see why the repentant churches might be tempted to fall into the large group of recluse churches?

I wonder if the recluse churches conclude that it's best to be silent on this matter because they would surely lose souls in the process or keep souls from coming to them. What congregation that wants to be faithful to God's Word isn't fearful of that?

But God doesn't ask us to worry about saving souls. He really doesn't. He simply asks us to preach his Word and let him worry about who is saved, for he promises that not one of his own can be taken from him. Not one of the elect will be lost (John 10:27–28; Romans 8:30).

On the flipside, if the recluse churches don't say anything on this matter, how will those who support the LGBT issue come to hear the gospel and be saved among them? How will fellow Christians, paralyzed by the topic, find a way out from under it themselves or rescue loved ones who struggle? How will such churches be faithful in sharing all of God's Word? Maybe these churches don't speak on LGBT issues because the arguments from the world have caught them off guard, and they don't have the right words to speak. Perhaps the instruction in many of these churches is minimal, leaving them with little understanding from the Scriptures on how to approach the subject in an evangelical way.

To such churches, I hope the thoughts contained in this book can be a voice in the spirit of Mordecai, Esther's cousin: "Do not think that because you are in the king's house you alone ... will escape. For if you remain silent at this time, relief and deliverance ... will arise from another place ... Who knows but that you have come to royal position for such a time as this?" (Esther 4:13-14).

I also hope that the message of this work will go on to provide an approach to speak to the issue at hand from a Scriptural point of view. In this book, there is a Scriptural approach to understanding the issues involved and answering many of the arguments Christians face. In the end, we are called to always be prepared to give an answer for the hope we have—and with all love, gentleness, and respect (1 Peter 3:15). We can't remain silent.

A Shibboleth for the Churches of Our Day[57]

In the book of Judges, chapter 12, you can read about a leader of God's people named Jephthah. He was a social outcast because his mother was a prostitute, and he himself was known to hang out with thugs. He was the kind of guy that would not have been received by the radical churches. Certainly his mother would not. Nevertheless, God, by his grace, lifted up this man, just as he wants to do with all LGBTs, a community that can never truly be lifted up by the rainbow churches. God empowered Jephthah to find his rightful place as a leader and deliverer of God's people.

Sadly, as Jephthah sought help from God's people in order to be delivered from their enemies, one group refused. They were the Ephraimites, a tribe of Israel, a group among God's people. Regardless, the Lord saw to it that Jephthah would have the victory, with or without the help of this tribe.

Later, when the Ephraimites learned that Jephthah had led all the other tribes of God's people to war against the enemy of Israel without them, they were upset. The Ephraimites threatened Jephthah's life, because he had put them in jeopardy when facing off with their

---

[57] Shibboleth – a peculiarity of pronunciation, behavior, mode of dress, etc., that distinguishes a particular class or set of persons. (http://dictionary.reference.com/browse/shibboleth?s=t)

enemy. (I suppose the downward spiraling of this LGBT issue and the worldly support of it is our modern-day enemy, but the souls entrapped there certainly are not. Those souls are never the enemy in our time of grace.)

In defense of his life, Jephthah fought against Ephraim, his brothers, and drove them back beyond the boundary of their land, beyond the Jordan River. As a result, this tribe couldn't return to their own land and the life they'd once had. The problem, however, was that this was only a temporary solution. Eventually the Ephraimites would slip through to again cause trouble among the people of God.

To permanently keep the wayward tribe in check, Jephthah's men devised a plan. In order to recognize the Ephraimites who would surely try to sneak back and blend in with God's people, Jephthah's men patrolled the fords of the Jordan. They would let no one pass unless they said a special word, "Shibboleth."

Jephthah and his men recognized that the word *Shibboleth* was a word the people of Ephraim could not pronounce correctly. The harsher "sh" sound was something they could not say. They replaced it with a simple "s" sound. So Jephthah's men demanded that anyone desiring to cross back into God's country say that one word. In having to say the word, the Ephraimites' lisp gave them away, and they were identified as the outsiders. Everyone could tell by this one word who was on God's side and who wasn't.

Maybe this book could be a Shibboleth on this issue among the churches. Beloved of the Lord, speak to your loved ones and Christian friends and ask if they hold to the truths contained in *Rainbow Savior*. If they haven't read it, offer them your copy of it or similar resources that speak the same. (If we are going to turn the tide on this issue and a host of others, the spread of God's Word among the churches is our only hope.)

If the response comes back that they don't believe that *Rainbow Savior* is in line with God's Word, ask them to show you where and why. I'm confident that they will not be able to show you from the Scriptures. Those who would not agree with the Scriptural truths

Rainbow Savior

of this work will show themselves to be either among the rainbow churches or the radical ones. At least they won't be able to remain in the camp of the recluse churches any longer.

If you have opportunity and can advance the conversation with them, ask them to share the thoughts of this work with the leaders of their congregations. All Christians would do well to know what their churches teach on homosexuality these days. It will serve as a litmus test for how they view God's Word and how they view essential concepts like sin and grace.

If we could accomplish this, we would begin to see what so many churches' true colors are. This "Shibboleth" test would identify and confirm congregations that are truly blessed to have the truth on this most devastating of issues. Not only that, but it may be a great help to any wayward churches, if they will listen.

All churches line up with the radical kind, the rainbow kind, the truly welcoming kind (repentance), or the recluse churches. Let the goal among Christian people be to turn everyone to the true church God gave, the churches that offer redemption in Christ on his terms and not on anybody else's. Tragically, the hour seems to be growing late for repentance churches like ours. More and more, they seem to be less and less.

God's people ought to give such churches their full support and continue to ensure that they remain faithful to all the Bible's teachings, all the Scriptures, to Christ himself. Perhaps this work in the hands of God's people, like you, could help to begin reforming the other wayward churches and embolden them to join the faithful ones. Whatever the case, thanks be to God that his true church still remains and can never fail!

11

Sweet Land of Liberty

The Land of the Free

It's a free country. We pride ourselves in that. It may very well be that, for the extent of our freedom, we are arguably the most blessed country in the world today. We believe in life, liberty, and the pursuit of happiness for everybody. We are so bold as to declare that this freedom is our inalienable right, granted to us by our Creator (Declaration of Independence). And yet, beloved of the Lord, we are now at a time in our country when religious liberties are being pitted against what others refer to as civil rights for the LGBT community.

How do we, as a congregation, speak lovingly to this issue and prove to others that we truly don't want to keep any freedoms from anybody? How do we express to the LGBT community that we do believe in equality, that we want all to be treated the same, even as we refrain from promoting sin? Finally, how can we look to preserve our religious liberties, which enable us to faithfully proclaim the law and gospel to everyone?

It is for these specific LGBT issues—now political matters—that I will look to address the general concept of freedom in this section and will focus more intently on the institution of marriage in the next. Be sure of this: the issues of true freedom, equality, civil rights, and the institution of marriage do speak to religious truths that we hold dear. These matters also impact how we practice our faith in this country. They are all "God issues." They are not just political matters to be recklessly abandoned to the government and whatever political parties dominate the political scene of our day.

The Return to Slavery

There was a time in this country when we were not all free. Our African-American brothers and sisters were forced to wear the shackles of slavery and bear an intolerable burden that no one should ever have to endure. The United States went on to pay a high price for such a societal sin when the Civil War alone claimed over half a million lives from the north and the south over this one issue. Finally, the slaves were set free under President Lincoln, a president who joined a multitude of other servicemen in paying the highest price for freedom.

Ever since those days that tested us as a country, our African-American brothers and sisters have been taking up their rights – rights that we as a country declare to be for all people by divine providence. What a tragedy if any of us should allow a return of slavery or enslavement for any of our fellow citizens, no matter what form of bondage it takes. We should not be so naïve to think that the threat of slavery came to an end at the conclusion of the Civil War. Slavery can still exist. It can come back in various ways. Personally, I fear it is already on the rise again, although in a different form. Not only has it returned, but I believe it is starting to thrive once more.

Jesus talked about the kind of slavery that now threatens us and will always threaten America or any other country. In John 8:34–36, we read, "Truly, truly, I say to you, everyone who practices sin is a slave to sin. The slave does not remain in the house forever; the son remains forever. So if the Son sets you free, you will be free indeed."

The people Jesus was speaking to didn't care to hear his words. They reasoned that they were a free people due to their lineage. They argued that they had never been enslaved by anyone because of their heritage, so it would be impossible to be enslaved now. They were offended that Jesus would call their carefree living—though it was riddled with countless new and ever-changing laws—a form of the deadliest kind of slavery. Do you see any parallels today?

If we think the slavery of sin is hardly any real kind of slavery at all, or that it's just a religious idea, we might want to rethink things a little. Even secular historians and statesmen have suggested that entire societies have collapsed from issues of immorality (sin). In speaking of the decline of the Roman Republic, Cicero, a statesman and historian (106–43 BC), said that his present generation had lost the substance of their republic because of their own moral failings. He lamented the fact that they had departed from their ancient customs and that there were no more men of virtue to preserve the old way of life and the institutions of their forefathers (Republic Book 5, opening paragraphs). Slavery to sin can bring the downfall of a nation, not just individuals.

Tacitus, another historian following the fall of the Roman Republic (AD 56–117), would prompt modern historians to make a similar connection between moral decay and societal decline, just as Cicero had done.

Edward Gibbon (AD 1737–1794), known as the first modern historian of ancient Rome, theorized that Rome fell largely because of a lack of civic virtue among its people.[58] He argued that their decadence created a vacuum for other forces to sweep through, making a once invincible empire nothing more than a buried page in world history. Gibbon's work weighs heavily on primary sources such as Tacitus' *The Histories*, which is filled with depictions of Rome as being full of sex, violence, and corruption at the highest levels. Though historians argue that a society's downfall has many more factors, I don't believe any would argue that morality is of

---

[58] *The History of the Decline and Fall of the Roman Empire.*

no consequence to a society's preservation. Sin is devastating to a people, not just individuals.

Whether or not moral decay was the downfall of Rome, the Scriptures tell us that decadence played a major role in the enslavement of the country of Judah (586 BC). Judah was carried off into captivity as a result of immorality that stemmed from a society immersed in idolatry. Immorality always originates from some form of idolatry.

Isaiah gave the reason for Judah's exile into Babylon and subsequent captivity in the following prophecy:

> Ah, sinful nation, a people laden with iniquity, offspring of evildoers, children who deal corruptly! ... If the LORD of hosts had not left us a few survivors, we should have been like Sodom, and become like Gomorrah. Hear the word of the LORD, you rulers of Sodom! Give ear to the teaching of our God, you people of Gomorrah! (Isaiah 1:4, 9-10)
>
> Their land is filled with silver and gold, and there is no end to their treasures; their land is filled with horses, and there is no end to their chariots. Their land is filled with idols; they bow down to the work of their hands, to what their own fingers have made. (Isaiah 2:7–8)
>
> The look on their faces bears witness against them; they proclaim their sin like Sodom; they do not hide it. (Isaiah 3:9)
>
> The daughters of Zion are haughty and walk with outstretched necks, glancing wantonly with their eyes, mincing along as they go, tinkling with their feet ... In that day the Lord will take away the finery of the anklets, the headbands, and the crescents; the pendants, the bracelets, and the scarves; the headdresses, the armlets, the sashes, the perfume boxes, and the amulets; the signet rings and nose rings; the festal robes, the mantles, the cloaks, and the handbags; the mirrors, the linen garments, the turbans,

and the veils. Instead of perfume there will be rottenness; and instead of a belt, a rope; and instead of well-set hair, baldness; and instead of a rich robe, a skirt of sackcloth; and branding instead of beauty. (Isaiah 3:16-24)

Woe to those who join house to house, who add field to field, until there is no more room ... The LORD of hosts has sworn in my hearing: "Surely many houses shall be desolate, large and beautiful houses, without inhabitant." (Isaiah 5:8–9)

Woe to those who rise early in the morning, that they may run after strong drink, who tarry late into the evening as wine inflames them! They have lyre and harp, tambourine and flute and wine at their feasts, but they do not regard the deeds of the LORD ... Therefore my people go into exile. (Isaiah 5:11-13)

Woe to those who call evil good and good evil, who put darkness for light and light for darkness, who put bitter for sweet and sweet for bitter! Woe to those who are wise in their own eyes, and shrewd in their own sight! (Isaiah 5:20–21)

Jesus warned of the danger of the slavery that binds those who practice immorality. Immoral living is a sign of a rejection of the Creator who endowed us with the inalienable right to be free. If we reject the Creator's design, then how can we believe that we will be able to keep our freedoms? How will we not lose our land of liberty? We do not retain our freedoms by the philosophy of "live and let live." That's precisely how we lose them. We can only escape the slavery of sin if the truth about its danger and the only Savior's solution sets us free (John 8:32).

Civil Rights

Since our society today is moved to talk about the present LGBT issue in terms of a civil rights movement—a movement for equal freedom for LGBTs—I would be remiss if I didn't speak to that idea. I especially would not be a faithful shepherd to you if I didn't address this topic from the Scriptures, since God's precious people are also being bombarded with a message of support for homosexuality in terms of civil rights.

God's people always do well to be informed, especially on matters as sensitive as the gay movement. If we don't know what people are fighting for, we can only lose credibility in the eyes of those who hold to such positions in our society. If we know the arguments, however, we are better equipped to understand where people are coming from, to have compassion on them, and to meet them where they are in order to lead them to Christ. If we are familiar with the movement and what the Scriptures ultimately say, we also won't be deceived by any worldly arguments and inadvertently become bound by sin ourselves. What follows is a simple summary of what many people are fighting for when it comes to the issue of gay rights.[59]

Basic Rights and Liberties

> The ACLU works to ensure that LGBT people have equal opportunity to participate fully in civil society. No LGBT person should experience discrimination in employment, housing, or in businesses and public places, or the suppression of their free expression or privacy rights. The ACLU seeks new laws against discrimination in states and at the federal level, and resists all attempts to weaken the impact of existing nondiscrimination laws. With the repeal

---

[59] https://www.aclu.org/lgbt-rights

of "Don't Ask, Don't Tell," our current federal priority is passage of the Employment Non-Discrimination Act.

Parenting

Fighting restrictions on parenting by LGBT people is critical because this discrimination causes serious, enduring harm to the lives of LGBT people and their children. The ACLU challenges policies and laws that prevent qualified and caring LGBT people from foster parenting or adopting kids. We also strive to change laws or practices that interfere in custody and visitation relationships between LGBT parents and their children. Our work debunks myths about the undesirability of same-sex couples raising children—myths often heard in the nationwide debate over marriage.

Relationships and Marriage

The ACLU believes that LGBT people, like everyone else, should have the freedom to build the kinds of personal, intimate relationships most meaningful to them without risking that their families will be disregarded or harmed by the state. Our goal is to obtain full recognition of same-sex relationships through marriage, in every state and at the federal level. In some states, the ACLU works for domestic partnership protections as a first step towards the full recognition and complete protections offered only by marriage.

Youth and Schools

The Youth and Schools program strives to make public schools and other state institutions for young people safe and bias-free for LGBT kids and teachers. We team up with students to fight for their free expression rights, to establish gay-straight alliances, and to advocate that LGBT kids be able to attend school dances with same-sex dates and dressed in gender nonconforming ways if they choose. We believe that all kids should be taught in an environment respectful of their sexual orientation and gender identity.

Discrimination against Transgender People

The ACLU strives to eliminate discrimination against transgender and gender nonconforming people and to create a society in which the full range of gender identities and expressions is respected and affirmed. We focus our efforts on ending discrimination in employment, housing, public accommodations, parenting, and schools. We also challenge legal barriers to transgender people obtaining government identity documents appropriate for their gender identity. Through our legal work, we help transgender people better understand their emerging legal rights and develop public education campaigns to persuade the general public about the importance of treating transgender people fairly.

As was highlighted through Jesus' words earlier in this chapter in John 8, an LGBT movement toward more rights is actually a movement toward more bondage to sin. There's no freedom in that at all. How unloving it would be for the Christian who is free to stand idly by allowing others to become victims to the slavery of sin! Spiritually speaking, where is the promotion of rights and equality in that?

At the same time, we Christian people are in a difficult spot. We need to tread lightly in this area of civil rights; otherwise, people may misunderstand us and perceive that we do not believe in the equality of all people. Make no mistake, the Bible declares us all to be equal before the Lord, and therefore we should be equally treated. In regard to loving others, the Christian is not to discriminate against people. God himself shows no favoritism (Romans 2:6–11). According to the Scriptures, though, equality for all does not mean that Christians should support anyone who pursues living contrary to God's will and, in that, pursues destruction.

So, what should God's people do? Ultimately, if people in our society choose to speak in terms of civil rights in regard to homosexuality, I will strive to dedicate myself to a couple of things: I will look to simply preach the fullness of God's Word faithfully to all who will listen, and I will live out what God's Word says in my life. As a citizen of this country, because I love my neighbor for Christ's sake, I will also look to uphold whatever I can that is found in the natural law God has put into all our hearts. I will do this for the one purpose of preserving peace so that the gospel of Christ might more easily go out into the world.

What might my neighborly deeds look like as a Christian and citizen of this country? I will pray for Christians in our society, especially those who serve in more visible ways as public servants. I will pray that our efforts as Christians to preserve God's natural law would prevail and that those opposing God's natural law would not be successful in their efforts. This is in keeping with one of the great petitions in the Lord's Prayer: "Your will be done on earth as it is in heaven" (Matthew 6:10). I will also look to do whatever I can in my actions as a citizen of this country to help be both "salt and light" in the public square (Matthew 5:13–14). All of this I will set out to do for one purpose: that the gospel would be heard and souls would be saved (1 Timothy 2:1–8).

In regard to our actions as a Christian people—people who are at odds with the world on this and many other issues—allow me to share with you one important biblical principle to guide us in the lives we live out in the world. It's a principle that is to be understood in light of another Scriptural truth: we are to act to the glory of God in all things, pointing others to Christ in everything. All the while, we should seek never to violate our own consciences or the consciences of weak brothers (1 Corinthians 10:23–33).

Wise as Serpents and Innocent as Doves (Matthew 10:16)

Remember Samuel. Samuel was a prophet of Israel who was tasked with the job of anointing a successor for wicked King Saul while Saul was still alive (1050–1010 BC). Samuel was concerned that Saul would ask him why he was going off to Bethlehem—where God had called Samuel to go to anoint David as king—so the prophet asked the Lord what he should say.

The Lord told him to simply tell Saul that he was going to that small town to sacrifice (1 Samuel 16:1–2). In other words, the Lord told Samuel, *"Don't reveal all the details of your business to a nonbeliever, because he will only despise my will."* Indeed, King Saul, in hearing of Samuel's mission, would have only trampled over that precious truth as swine only trample over pearls (Matthew 7:6).

Remember Naaman. Naaman was the commander of the army of Aram at the time of Elisha the prophet (890–830 BC). He was cleansed of his leprosy by Elisha, and in hearing the gospel of God, Naaman became a believer in the true God. Before returning home, he told the prophet that his service to the king required him to escort his pagan king to a temple of a false god and kneel beside him.

Elisha answered, "Go in peace" (2 Kings 5:18–19). In other words, Elisha said, *"Just because you kneel down in service to a nonbeliever in his nonbelieving purpose, this does not mean you have violated God's law."*

Remember Shadrach, Meshach, and Abednego. Shadrach, Meshach, and Abednego were faithful believers in the land of their captivity. Being the gifted men that they were, those three men were forced into the service of their captor's kingdom along with the prophet Daniel (605–537 BC). But when King Nebuchadnezzar made a decree that all should bow in worship to a ninety-foot idol of his own invention, these three brave souls—*in order not to deny Christ—refused to obey their ruler, even on penalty of death* (Daniel 3).

Regarding this last example, if a Christian should have to lose everything, let it not be for the issue of homosexuality, which, in the end, is only a side issue! This sin among wayward people is merely one of many symptoms of a people without faith in Jesus Christ, the Savior of us all. Therefore, if we must lose everything, let us lose all things for what's most important: our certain hope that Jesus is the Christ and that he alone will, by faith in him, raise us from the grave.

We need to take opportunity to let everyone know that faith in Jesus as the Christ, the only Savior of the world, is the only issue we have. Isn't that the reason that Jesus ultimately gave himself over to death when accused of all sorts of things in the trial of his life? The only time Jesus gave an answer when he was accused was on the one question of whether or not he was the Messiah. It was to that alone that he finally spoke, and it was for that alone that they crucified him (Luke 22:66–71).

In other situations, when people were looking to trap Jesus on mere side issues, Jesus wisely avoided entrapment, all for the sake of the gospel (Matthew 21:23–27; 22:15–22 about John's baptism and Caesar's coin). Like Christ, the only thing the apostle Paul would admit to when he was on trial was that he stood accused solely for his hope in Christ and the resurrection from the dead (Acts 24:21).

The gospel is the main cause for which Christians are to sacrifice themselves in dealing with a nonbelieving world, and it should be the sole reason we forfeit our livelihood or lives—if we must—regardless of the reason we are put on trial.[60] The cause in all this is for the sake

---

[60] Any Christian business owner or employee should speak on this issue with great caution. Why harm or destroy one's own business unnecessarily, and at the same time endanger having other opportunities to provide a witness to Christ in words and actions? If one can avoid speaking to this issue directly in connection with his business or profession, it may indeed save the Christian much undue grief. Let the Christian be wise and remain innocent!

of lost souls in the world who war against us. The weapon we use is God's Word alone, which is the weapon of true love.

In regard to being "wise as serpents and innocent as doves," perhaps a particular word would prove helpful to Christians among us who serve in civil government. I am especially thinking about Christian politicians, although the following counsel would serve as a guide for any Christian speaking on the divisive topic of homosexuality to the nonbelieving world.[61] To be wise in politics is to speak the language of the public square, which is not the Word of God but human reason. That may sound surprising to us Christians, but it's true. Please, hear me out.

For any Christian to appeal to the Bible as authoritative among nonbelievers in our day and age is as useless as if someone started speaking to them in Latin. The people of this world simply will not understand that the Bible is enough for the Christian, and the politician may very well be in danger of losing credibility when directly citing the Word of God to substantiate his or her position. In terms of secular government, the most important thing for the Christian to remember is that God has not called for the politician or any in government to be keepers of the gospel and establish God's kingdom through that institution. The mission of spreading the gospel has been given to the holy Christian church alone (1 Peter 2:9). Just as we would not want the church to "bear the sword" of the government (Romans 13:1–7), so we would not want the government to act as if it is Christ's kingdom on earth (John 18:36).[62]

---

[61] Before a school board, in a coffee shop with nonbelieving friends, around a holiday table with nonbelieving family, the Christian is cautioned to speak with all love, gentleness, and respect so as not to lose an opportunity to share the gospel. Many times, it may be best to not speak at all, in the hopes of keeping a line open for the greater cause of the gospel.

[62] Western history, from the time of Constantine (AD 300s) to the end of the Holy Roman Empire (early AD 1800s), is full of examples of why it is ungodly to mix the powers of church and state. Mixing the purposes of the two very different kingdoms is not God's will, as surely as Christ proclaimed that his kingdom is not of this world (John 18:36).

Inside and outside a political career, the Christian is to give testimony to Christ, but in the business of civil government, wise arguments will be put forth on the basis of human reason. Thankfully, the instructed Christian is best qualified for such a task, because the Christian's human reason, which must be schooled in the Scriptures, is sanctified by the Word of God. Whereas the world can only struggle to distinguish right from wrong—and often fails in whole or in part due to warped consciences and flawed understanding of the natural knowledge of God's law—the Christian who is well versed in the Word can only succeed. Still, arguments of the Christian's sanctified reason are to come off as just that: human reason.

For instance, in the public square, instead of saying that gay marriage is a sin according to God's Word—which it is—one would be wiser to declare rightfully that traditional marriage has served society well over the history of humankind when not abused, and since it forms an essential fabric of stability for society, it is for society's good that it remain unchanged. Redefining marriage, therefore, is unreasonable and dangerous to the foundation of society. Marriage is not an institution with which to tamper. It is not a place to test out other kinds of unions. I'm sure there are even better arguments for sanctified human reason that can be utilized. The Christian politician is encouraged to find them and use them with all gentleness, love, and respect!

Truly, we need more Christians in politics and government, especially those who can handle politics in a wise manner but remain innocent! Truly, we Christians are at an advantage above all others, because we know that the Word of God is true! Therefore, sanctified reason will be able to find a way to point to the evidence of the goodness of God's law in this life without directly referring to God or the Scriptures to people who would only trample over those truths anyway.

This wise approach of the Christian in civil government, of course, is all for the purpose of maintaining order in society so that Christians, as the church, can bring in the Word of God and the gospel in the hopes of seeing God's kingdom established in the hearts of people. Ultimately, the Christian civil leader needs to be able to distinguish clearly between the missions of the two kingdoms—earthly kingdoms (Romans 13:1–7) and God's heavenly kingdom (Matthew 28:18–20).[63]

Let me share one last thought on civil rights before we move along. I am concerned that there is one American right that we might not all be able to exercise in the near future. If we are going to speak in terms of a civil rights movement, I would be inclined to speak about the freedom of religion and religious liberties, which are now at stake. Up to this time in our country, it's been everyone's right to practice religion freely and to speak our minds freely. We have freedom of religion and freedom of speech (US Constitution, Bill of Rights, Amendment I).

Presently, I have the right to publish a Scriptural point of view on LGBT issues for God's people. I fear that in a generation or two, if not in my own generation, a person will no longer be able to publish a book like this. I wonder who might even publish a work like this now, considering the content of this chapter and some others, whether a Christian publisher or secular. It's too divisive a topic already.

What do you think? Are our religious rights in jeopardy due to the issue at hand? Is my confession of my belief, which is offered to the church and opposes homosexual behavior on Scriptural grounds, soon to be outlawed in the public square? As the apostle Paul once did as a Roman citizen, I believe people like me would be wise to appeal to "Caesar" all the more (Acts 26:6) to protect the right to preach the

---

[63] The line of thinking shared here regarding the Christian in civil government comes from Professor Daniel M. Deutschlander's work: "Civil Government: God's Other Kingdom." It is an excellent read and highly recommended for all Christians at this time, especially civil servants! His other works "The Narrow Lutheran Middle" and "Theology of the Cross" are also excellent reads and a must for every Christian. Search for them at www.nph.net.

fullness of the Word of God and the gospel publicly.[64] In the end, this is what's at stake on this issue.

Consider, then, my words here to be written with the cause of the gospel alone in mind. Humanly speaking, the good news about Jesus needs some semblance of peace in society for it to spread more quickly (1 Timothy 2:1–4). The Savior's voice becomes harder to hear when the church is persecuted publicly on any given issue. However, if one day I should be denied the public right to preach the Word of God in all its fullness and the gospel, so be it. We must obey God rather than men, no matter the cost (Acts 5:29). Souls need the gospel, whether or not it is a crime to preach it.

Bullying

It seems we hear so much about bullying these days in our society, especially in schools—more than I recall while growing up. I get the sense that our society is really intent now on stopping it at every turn. I'm truly glad about an effort to end all bullying, and at the same time, it gives me pause to wonder about what may lie ahead for the Christian in regard to homosexuality.

As to bullying, it saddens me that anyone would be picked on or persecuted for anything. Having been bullied when I was young, I know how frightening it is. I know the anxious thoughts that come with it. I know the thoughts of revenge. I know the thoughts of despair. I know how these things consume those bullied. My heart is truly troubled whenever I hear of someone, a young person especially, who doesn't want to live anymore because they feel like they can never escape the grip of a bully. How it saddens me greatly

---

[64] What a great need there is for Christians to serve as leaders in civil government to protect the church's rights to free speech and freedom of religion. Only let Christian leaders in society wisely protect these rights and all other rights on the basis of sanctified human reason!

when individuals decide to take their own lives because they believe it's the only way out.

Should I come to find someone who is being bullied, the love of Christ compels me to step in as a Christian and stand up for that person like our Savior did for all of us. It goes without saying, then, that bullying is to be beyond the realm of possibility for the Christian. Frankly, it's not possible to bully and to keep faith in Christ (1 John 4:20). Such a person should hardly be considered a follower of Christ. What does Christ have to do with bullying? The two have as much in common as light does with darkness. Anyone who claims to be a Christian yet chooses to bully a gay person should be put outside of the church if he refuses to repent and turn from such a sin as that. Apologies should be given immediately from such a one, and a life of bearing fruits of repentance should follow in the shadow of the cross.

As a Christian pastor, I would look to be there for any who are bullied and who identify themselves as being gay. I would say to them, "You don't deserve to be treated like this. You have a Savior who poured out his blood for you, who in that act says that you are more precious than anything else in God's eyes." I would do all that I could to see them safe. Again, isn't this what Jesus did for all of us?

Though I would neither support that person's sexual preferences nor his acting out upon them, I would see such a soul as God does—equally loved and equally desperate to be loved. I'd see him no differently from the way the Lord looks at me. If I had opportunity, I would hope to point that person to a happier way than the homosexual lifestyle can offer. I'd look to share with them the Word, about a holy life that is granted to all by the work of Christ Jesus on the cross, a life that can never be snuffed out.

In return, I would hope to find the same kind of respect for my views, no matter who disagreed with me—and not just for me either. I would hope that all who are like you and me would be treated fairly as we send our children to public or private schools, as we seek employment and work in the world, as we create our own businesses, and as we offer our services to the public with the desire to keep our consciences clear before God. I would hope to see that, though others may disagree with our belief in the Scriptures, we could have a civil conversation over this issue, nothing more or less.

Whatever the case, our Savior was bullied for speaking the truth in love. To one who struck Jesus for his words, Jesus said, "If what I said is wrong, bear witness about the wrong; but if what I said is right, why do you strike me?" (John 18:23). The bullies of the world were the ones who crucified Jesus for the things he preached. They didn't even let up when he was on the cross (Matthew 27:42). But by this he taught us, "It is enough for the disciple to be like his teacher, and the servant like his master. If they have called the master of the house Beelzebul [the Devil], how much more will they malign those of his household" (Matthew 10:25).

I'm at peace with being bullied for holding to the Scriptures (1 Peter 2:19–23). I'm committed to turning the other cheek, so help me God (Matthew 5:38–48). I want to encourage you, God's flock, to keep the same Scriptural attitude, no matter where you find yourself—whether at home, in the workplace, at school, or in the public square. It is good to suffer for doing right (1 Peter 2:20–21).

Speaking the truth in love to the LGBT community for their benefit is worth any bullying that may come. It's worth the risk to reach enslaved souls to set them free. It's worth being ridiculed, accosted, fired, imprisoned, or even put to death. That goes for me, you, and our children after us.

Jesus thought that facing death was worth it, and because he did, we can all be free. Like Christ, we Christians should be willing to pay the ultimate price for anyone trapped in slavery. Let us only speak the truth in love, keeping the gospel as the main cause in all things; and let us care for all people, wherever we can, whether they are gay or straight.

Rev. William A. Monday

True Freedom

As we think of the freedoms we enjoy in this sweet land of liberty, I would like to ask one last question: are we becoming a freer people or a more enslaved people? I suppose that depends on how we all are defining freedom these days. If we define freedom as the right to do anything we want, including what's wrong, I think we all can agree that's not real freedom. Freedom is never the ability to do what is evil and then call it good. Jesus says that's slavery (John 8:32).

Beloved of the Lord, don't be deceived. Even if we hear shouts in the streets for more freedoms, let's remember how Jesus defined it. The true definition of real freedom has always been the ability to do what's right, even if it may seem more pleasurable to do what's wrong (Galatians 5:13).

Are we losing our freedoms and becoming ever more entrapped by the shackles of sin? Our forefathers could teach us something about the real cause of freedom in the hymn they designated for the people of this sweet land of liberty. It's a hymn worth singing from time to time among God's people, especially as we hope to witness to our fellow citizens across the land about true freedom.

> Glory, glory! Hallelujah! Glory, glory! Hallelujah!
> Glory, glory! Hallelujah! His Truth is marching on.
> In the beauty of the lilies Christ was born across the sea,
> With a glory in his bosom that transfigures you and me.
> As he died to make men holy, let us live to make men free,
> While God is marching on.
>
> —"Battle Hymn of the Republic," refrain and verse 5

12

Marriage Redefined

Moses and Marriage

In November 2012 Minnesotans went to the polls to cast votes on a proposed amendment to the state constitution, which, had it passed, would have defined marriage the traditional way: as a union between one man and one woman. The amendment's passage failed by a slight minority (48 percent).[65]

Can you believe that the state legislature passed a law to legalize same-sex marriage some six months later in the spring of 2013? It's a rarity to see the government move so quickly on anything, and especially on an issue that bears such a close division among its citizens (greater than 48 percent to less than 52 percent). What surprised me more than this was that there were those among the

---

[65] http://www.huffingtonpost.com/2012/11/07/minnesota-amendment-1-results-2012_n_2050310.html. Keep in mind too that the nature of voting on this particular issue wasn't entirely clear to some voters. Any "none" votes were actually counted as votes against adopting the amendment to preserve traditional marriage. Also, some people wonder if the voters misunderstood the amendment about marriage. Some voters may have perceived that a "new amendment" about marriage was intended to introduce same-gender marriage, when the exact opposite was the case. Similarly, voters may have believed that in voting "yes," they were adopting same-gender marriage, and that by voting "no," they were intending to preserve traditional marriage. Again, the exact opposite was the case.

voters who claimed to be Christian,[66] who voted down the amendment for traditional marriage. Even more shocking to me was the fact that, among the state legislators, there were so-called Christians who voted to legalize same-sex marriage. I wondered how this could be.

One of the arguments I've heard in support of redefining marriage is that the Bible is no longer relevant on this issue. It's an argument raised by both nonbelievers and, sadly, an ever-increasing number of Christians-in-name. (Up to this point in our discussion, however, it is perfectly clear that the Bible is relevant to the topic of homosexuality and that it always applies when it comes to the preservation of traditional marriage.) Still, some within the visible church strive to prove their argument of the Bible's irrelevancy by pointing out that there are many Old Testament laws which no longer apply. The implication drawn from this idea is that the biblical law on traditional marriage is no longer applicable. In the end, it seems that many so-called Christians have bought into the idea that legalizing same-gender marriage is the more enlightened and loving thing to do in our day, rather than preserving traditional marriage.

All of this discussion about redefining marriage to legalize same-gender marriage reminds me of a dark time in the history of Israel in the days of Moses. There was a period of time when people in Moses' society believed that they could do with marriage whatever they thought best, regardless of God's original design for that institution. I'd like to share with you some words from an "amendment" to the constitution of Israel's society, which touches on that dark period. Most importantly, we will look to Jesus' very own words on this matter to explain to us that redefining marriage is never a good thing for any society. Every Christian needs to understand that.

---

[66] I do not mean to say that any Christian who is in favor of same-gender marriage cannot possibly know Christ or have saving faith. However, such a one cannot fully understand God's will on this matter and, as such, is in danger of losing saving faith and all that Christ has won for him by his sacrifice on the cross. Such a one is encouraged to return to the Scriptures.

Under inspiration and direction of the Lord, Moses declared the following allowance for marriage for his society:

> When a man takes a wife and marries her, if then she finds no favor in his eyes because he has found some indecency in her, and he writes her a certificate of divorce and puts it in her hand and sends her out of his house, and she departs out of his house, and if she goes and becomes another man's wife, and the latter man hates her and writes her a certificate of divorce and puts it in her hand and sends her out of his house, or if the latter man dies, who took her to be his wife, then her former husband, who sent her away, may not take her again to be his wife, after she has been defiled, for that is an abomination before the LORD. And you shall not bring sin upon the land that the LORD your God is giving you for an inheritance. (Deuteronomy 24:1–4)

What was the reason for Moses' words here in allowing for what we might call "no-fault" divorce—words that the Lord God gave him to write under a theocracy? What was happening in that society that would force such an allowance? And what was the Lord ultimately declaring about the people there? Jesus explains it all in Mark 10.

Jesus and Marriage

Once there was a crowd that gathered around Jesus. The crowd was asking the same kinds of questions about the Old Testament, Moses, and marriage that many of us are asking today. As is true in our day, many people had already made up their minds when they asked Jesus about the issue of redefining marriage. As they stood before Jesus, they didn't really care about what he actually had to say. If he didn't agree with them, they were only hoping to find a way to write him off and return to their lives of picking and choosing what they wanted to believe about the Bible. (Does this sound familiar?) We come across this incident in Mark 10:1–12.

> And Pharisees came up and in order to test him asked, "Is it lawful for a man to divorce his wife?" He answered them, "What did Moses command you?"
> They said, "Moses allowed a man to write a certificate of divorce and to send her away." And Jesus said to them, "Because of your hardness of heart he wrote you this commandment. But from the beginning of creation, 'God made them male and female. Therefore a man shall leave his father and mother and hold fast to his wife, and the two shall become one flesh.' So they are no longer two but one flesh. What therefore God has joined together, let not man separate."
> And in the house the disciples asked him again about this matter. And he said to them, "Whoever divorces his wife and marries another commits adultery against her, and if she divorces her husband and marries another, she commits adultery." (Mark 10:1–12)

Jesus sheds light on what was happening in the context of Deuteronomy 24. Because the people had become so perverse and rebellious, Moses had no other choice but to establish a law as a form of judgment and a curb to restrain evildoers as much as possible in regard to divorce. That, by the way, is a use of the law as a curb, as surely as the apostle Paul said that the law was made not for the righteous but for the wicked (1 Timothy 1:8–10). Furthermore, whereas Christians have not been inspired today, Moses was inspired to establish such a law directly by God, who alone can measure the hardness of a heart.

Anyone who claims to be a Christian and thinks it's permissible—and even loving—to tamper with marriage clearly does not know the

Scriptures. In reality, whether people recognize it or not, with the passage of such laws and allowances that redefine marriage, voters and legislators alike are condemning their fellow citizens. By these laws, voters and legislators are also proving themselves arrogant, because, by their actions, they are claiming divine knowledge and an ability to read the hearts of a people, declaring them to be beyond saving.

According to Jesus' own words, this was what Moses was doing, and it was only permissible for him because the Lord God had weighed the hearts of many and found them to be too hardened. By God's direction, Moses was serving as an agent of wrath in declaring an allowance for "no-fault" divorce. Christians today are not privileged to have this kind of divine revelation or inspired direction from God.

What's more disheartening is that those who claim to know Christ, yet pass new laws for same-gender marriage, are unaware of what their actions really mean. Did Christian voters or legislators in our society strike down traditional marriage and approve of same-gender marriage to invoke the curb use of the law? I'm confident nobody did. Who would dare admit it, if they had, and how would such an act be justifiable or even serve as a curb?

Therefore, let nonbelievers be the ones to pervert the laws of the land, establish same-gender marriage, and warrant divine judgment with increasing speed. As for Christians, let us only establish or preserve laws that protect things like traditional marriage for the benefit of society and stave off impending judgment as long as we can. In short, it is never a good sign when a society redefines marriage.

LGBTs and Marriage

There are those in the LGBT community who would agree with me that redefining marriage would only be harmful to others. Were you aware of that? It's for reasons different from the reason that the Scriptures say, but it's interesting to note.

There are presently two schools of thought on gay marriage among LGBT leaders. One school of thought continues to pursue what they call "equal rights in marriage" so that the LGBT community as a whole might be recognized as equal to everybody else and so that people might marry whomever they love. Most supporters of gay marriage seem to hold to that view. They believe that a redefinition of marriage can only benefit gay people. The other school of thought, which runs contrary to legalizing gay marriage, is that the traditional form of marriage is an oppressive institution, which would not serve the LGBT community well at all.

Paula Ettelbrick, a once prominent advocate for gay rights who is now deceased, said that marriage was a "wonderful institution, if you like living in institutions."[67] This sentiment of hers has somewhat impacted the present pursuit for gay marriage among LGBT leaders. Their purpose in pursuing marriage equality has an added feature: once the right is acquired, they intend to further change it and do away with the "oppressive nature" of the institution. This is part of the agenda for some LGBT advocates.

Paula Ettelbrick, who was originally opposed to redefining marriage to include gay people, has inspired in the minds of fellow advocates a pursuit of something more with marriage rights. She said, "Being queer is more than setting up house, sleeping with a person of the same gender, and seeking state approval for doing so ... Being queer means pushing the parameters of sex, sexuality, and family, and in the process, transforming the very fabric of society ... We must keep our eyes on the goal ... of radically reordering society's view of reality."[68]

Perhaps many in the LGBT community will be satisfied once the law of the land allows for gay marriage. This seems more and more inevitable across the fifty states, as one by one each state is changing.

---

[67] http://www.guardian.co.uk/world/2011/nov/03/paula-ettelbrick-obituary

[68] http://pegasus.rutgers.edu/~review/vol61n3/Stein_v61n3.pdf

But according to some proponents of same-sex marriage, that will only be the beginning of dismantling the institution entirely.

This is no secret agenda either. This is a pursuit that many are very open about, because they believe that marriage is simply oppressive, especially for women. I believe this is important for God's people to know. How is this not a critical issue for our society, especially as we come to understand the meaning God attached to marriage in the Holy Scriptures?

The Old Testament Laws (OT Laws) and Marriage

Let's return to the topic of Moses and marriage. I have noticed a popular approach to the Bible these days that is really nothing new. I share the following with you so that you are well defended against a prevailing but false approach to the Scriptures, employed by many who support homosexuality.

In the present debate on redefining marriage, people are pitting parts of the Bible against other parts. It's similar to what Jesus experienced with the Pharisees pitting Moses against marriage (Mark 10:1–12) or the Sadducees pitting marriage against the resurrection of the dead (Matthew 22:23–33). Just like the Pharisees and Sadducees, people today are looking to turn some Old Testament laws against the law of holy matrimony. For anyone who would do that, Jesus' words to the Sadducees are fitting: "You are wrong, because you know neither the Scriptures nor the power of God" (Matthew 22:29).

Admittedly, those words of Jesus are pointed, but we can at least understand why he was so serious. The Bible is the Word of God, and we are all lost if we look to use it according to our own personal preferences. We need to at least do the honest thing and approach the Scriptures in the way the Scriptures prescribe, or we must deny them altogether.

An invaluable rule for the interpretation of the laws of Moses comes from Jesus Christ and his disciples in the pages of the New

Testament. The general rule of thumb is this: whatever is commanded in the Old Testament must be repeated in the New Testament. This was the principle that Christ and his apostles followed for themselves.

The following categories of laws found in the Old Testament will be addressed by this rule of thumb. In the process, we will expose the error of pitting any of the Mosaic laws against marriage today. We would do well to remember this, should the inevitable argument arise for gay marriage that says, "The Old Testament has many laws that no longer apply, so why should laws against homosexuality be maintained?"

OT Laws Are "Guardians" (A Hedge)

When the apostle Paul was spreading the gospel of Jesus Christ, he ran into a group of people who struggled to believe that Jesus had fulfilled all the Law in order to earn all the righteousness God required of everybody. They were called the Judaizers. This group's beliefs fell somewhere between Judaism and Christianity. They wanted to believe in Jesus as the Savior, but they believed that they also had to appease God by keeping the Law God gave to Moses. It was a view that they were forcing on Christians.

The Judaizers made a big deal about the custom of circumcision, which was not only commanded under Moses but was given first to Abraham (Genesis 17), the father of the faith. You can read all about the situation Paul faced with the Judaizers in the book of Galatians.

The practice of circumcision marked the Old Testament people as a people separated for God. The practice drastically symbolized God cutting off the wicked world and wicked hearts from his people. It was an intense symbol of God doing away with all that was wrong and, as such, delivering a sanctified or holy people to himself. The religious terms *sanctify* and *holy* are synonyms that mean "set apart" (Deuteronomy 30:6; Romans 2:28–29). The meaning is derived from the Hebrew word for *holy* (*Kadosh*), which means to cleave or cut in two.

Rainbow Savior

In the imagery of separation, we now begin to see one important purpose of the Old Testament Law. Because the Jewish people had an important role to play in bringing the Savior into the world (Genesis 12:1–3), it was imperative that they remain distinct from all the other pagan nations. God gave them many unique laws to hedge them in or guard them from the world in keeping with their special purpose.

This plan of separation would also make the people of God stick out like a sore thumb among all the other nations. In drawing attention to the Jews with these laws, some from the Gentile world would, out of curiosity, seek to understand the reason for the Jews' separation. The Jews would be able to remind the Gentiles of the ancient promise made to all people concerning the Messiah—that the Savior of the world would come through the Jews (Genesis 3:15; 12:1–3). The salvation of both Jews and Gentiles was always God's desire (Isaiah 49:6).

Once Jesus came and fulfilled the requirements of God's Law for all people (Galatians 4:4), he set his own people free from those special guardian laws. Those laws had served their purpose. Like children who become adults and leave their guardians, so the followers of Jesus could now leave those laws that hedged them in.

In this freedom, God's people would no longer need to wait for the world to come to them, but they could go out into all the world to share the news of salvation. They would be so free that they could even take on all customs and practices for themselves that were not inherently sinful. In becoming like all others, some from the world could become sanctified like them through the gospel of Jesus Christ (1 Corinthians 9:19–23).

In reminding the Judaizers of this fulfilled purpose of the guardian laws, Paul said, "So then, the law was our guardian until Christ came, in order that we might be justified by faith. But now that faith has come, we are no longer under a guardian" (Galatians 3:24–25).

After the coming of Christ and the fulfillment of the Law, the following regulations were nullified, among other practices: making distinctions between clean and unclean food, like shellfish (Leviticus 11); wearing special clothing of only one kind (Deuteronomy 22:11); planting only one kind of seed in a field, and mating livestock of only one kind (Leviticus 19:19); boiling a young goat in its mother's milk or getting body markings and piercings (Deuteronomy 14:21; Leviticus 19:28).

Those laws were not given because the practices they forbade were in and of themselves sinful or timeless. They were forbidden for a time because the other nations were known for those practices (Leviticus 20:22–24), and if God's people became like everyone else in all they did, they would be in danger of becoming lost in the world. If there was no distinction between the Old Testament people and everyone else, that would have put the promise of the Messiah and salvation in jeopardy. After understanding the purpose of these laws, it is easy to see the separation theme running throughout them and the reason they no longer apply.

There are two examples of the apostles showing that these laws had been fulfilled and were therefore obviated, and they can be found in the New Testament. Peter's vision of unclean animals serves as the first proof (Acts 10:9–19). Through his vision, God declared all unclean animals clean to eat. By this, God was teaching Peter that the dividing hedge between Jews (clean) and Gentiles (unclean) had been knocked down by Christ (Ephesians 2:11–22). The subsequent conversion of Cornelius, a Gentile, in the presence of Peter was no accident (Acts 10:36–48).

The Jerusalem Council and an important decree from that apostolic body (Acts 15:20) serves as the second proof. In a special decree, the Jerusalem Council of apostles declared that all guardian laws were fulfilled and nullified. The decree would only go on to ask for one temporary concession among the Gentiles concerning the guardian or hedge laws. This concession asked Gentiles to refrain from eating meat that had been sacrificed to idols or strangled and having the blood still in it.

This request was not made because of the timeless nature of some law. It was based on the Jews' need to process the total freedom they had been given in Christ. A change of heart, attitudes, and practices often comes slowly. Paul showed that the decree from the Jerusalem Council only covered a short time, when he proclaimed that all meat was permissible to eat (1 Corinthians 8).

On the other hand, sexual immorality was still forbidden by the Jerusalem Council, and all the Scriptures are in agreement with this to this day, whether Old Testament or New. Although laws concerning immorality helped separate the Old Testament people from the world, they were never primarily under the guardian laws. The laws forbidding immorality fit better under another category, which we'll get to in a moment.

If you come across laws in the Old Testament that seem strange, you likely have stumbled upon guardian laws intended to safeguard the Old Testament people from the idolatrous influences of pagan nations. Those are no longer binding. Though strange to us, they served a vital purpose of guarding the people and keeping them distinct so that the Christ would be recognized. The heart of those laws still speaks to us as we consider that we should also separate ourselves from the world regarding whatever is sinful to God. People who pit these laws against marriage show they do not fully understand the Scriptures.

OT Laws Are Ceremonial

Another group of Old Testament laws that are no longer binding are ceremonial laws. Much of the order for worship as found in Leviticus fits this category. The ceremonial laws served the purpose of reflecting the people's broken relationship with God and the constant need to be reconciled, a reconciliation that would only come by sacrifice and the shedding of blood (Leviticus 17:11; Hebrews 9:22). From the Holy of Holies in the temple to the different kinds of sacrifices offered outside and all the festivals and procedures attached to them, these ceremonial places and regulations provided different pictures of the restoration Christ would bring one day in the shedding of his blood. Jesus alone would provide complete purification and reconciliation for his people to enter into the throne room of God (Hebrews 7–10).

The apostle Paul taught that the ceremonial laws had been fulfilled and were therefore obviated by Christ too. This includes what might be considered the highest of ceremonial laws, the Sabbath regulation (Hebrews 4). Paul wrote, "One person esteems one day as better than another, while another esteems all days alike. Each one should be fully convinced in his own mind. The one who observes the day, observes it in honor of the Lord" (Romans 14:5–6).

In another place he says the same thing, adding a little more detail: "When you were dead in your sins and in the uncircumcision of your flesh, God made you alive with Christ. He forgave us all our sins, having canceled the charge of our legal indebtedness ... Therefore do not let anyone judge you by what you eat or drink, or with regard to a religious festival, a New Moon celebration or a Sabbath day" (Colossians 2:13, 16).

Jesus too pointed out the ceremonial nature of the Sabbath law when he said, "The Sabbath was made for man, not man for the Sabbath" (Mark 2:27).

Since the reality of Christ has come, we no longer need the ceremonial images of him or his work in those laws which, by their design, pointed ahead to what Christ would be and do. Those laws were just as the Bible calls them, "shadows of things to come" (Colossians 2:17). Though these laws do not apply to us anymore, they still provide beautiful pictures of the kind of rest (*Sabbath* means "rest") the Savior has provided for his people. Anyone who pits these laws against marriage also shows that they do not fully understand the Scriptures.

OT Laws Are Civil

Another type of Old Testament law is known as civil law. This law pertained to the nation of Israel long ago, just as our civil laws pertain only to the nation of the United States of America today. We covered one of the civil laws already: Moses' allowance for no-fault divorce. That was for purely civil purposes.

Another popular law quoted from the Old Testament that belongs under civil law is this: "eye for an eye and tooth for a tooth" (Exodus 21:24). This was a law to ensure order and to curb societal violence, just as we have laws that do the same. This law looked to enforce justice in the face of wrongdoing by those in authority. If someone stole from you in Moses' day, the authorities were there to exact punishment equal to the crime.

Jesus showed that the "eye for an eye" law belonged to the civil authorities and not to individuals (vigilantes) when he proclaimed, "You have heard that it was said, 'An eye for an eye and a tooth for a tooth.' But I say to you, 'Do not resist the one who is evil. But if anyone slaps you on the right cheek, turn to him the other also'" (Matthew 5:38–39).

Vengeance is the Lord's (Romans 12:19), and it belongs to those to whom he's given that kind of authority (Romans 13:1–4). Citizens of a government are not to seek revenge but are to leave that to the state and to God as they themselves turn the other cheek. Citizens are only to submit to the governing authorities in all things (Romans 13:1), unless those governing authorities defy God (Acts 5:29). Even then, citizens may only display civil disobedience and must be willing to pay the price for whatever ungodly law of the land they refuse to keep (Daniel 3; Daniel 6).

Jesus was not contradicting Moses when he spoke on the civil law, "eye for an eye." This kind of clarification provided by Jesus was common and was similar to the clarification he delivered on divorce before his disciples. And these clarifications were necessary because, just as people do today, people in Jesus' day had been perverting the truth about the Mosaic Law.

In Moses' day the civil authority given to him was also passed down to leaders of the community, which included all parents (Deuteronomy 21:18–21). The leaders and parents were the police, judges, jurors, and executioners in those days. This is how God structured the form of government known in the Old Testament as a theocracy (1 Samuel 8:6–7). We might think it strange that religious leaders, parents, and elders were to carry out the death penalty for those guilty of idolatry (Exodus 22:20) or adultery, among other forms of immorality (Leviticus 20:10–12), but perhaps it is only strange to us because that's not how we do things in our society. As to any other civil laws that might initially offend us, a careful study of the context of that day will show why the laws were written as they were (Deuteronomy 22:22–30).[69]

Finally, before we're tempted to judge Old Testament society as being too harsh in regard to idolatry and adultery, couldn't we reason that idolatry under a theocracy is a form of treason? Would it be so strange to award the death penalty to someone who has committed treason? We do that in our country.

As to the breaking of marriage by adultery or immorality, is it so strange to make that a capital crime? After all, God said nothing was to separate a married couple but death (Matthew 19:6). Since he defined it that way, the death penalty would seem to fit the crime. We have simply become so accustomed to idolatry, divorce, and immorality in our day that we struggle to see how destructive and deadly these forms of sin are to us.

At the same time, we would do well to remember that God desires mercy, not punishment (Exodus 34:6–7). Just because a

---

[69] This God-given authority to government also includes the ability to wage war against other nations (Deuteronomy 20). The conquests of Joshua, and other wars in the Old Testament that God commanded, all fell under the civil laws and authorities God established for his divine purposes. Governmental authority is given to punish the wrongdoer and to deliver the righteous, whether it's the individual citizen or other nations (Romans 13:1–5).

crime carried a maximum sentence of death in the Old Testament, this doesn't mean it was always carried out (2 Samuel 12:13). In our day, in civil law, the maximum sentence is most often used as a deterrent. Who's to say this wasn't the case for the most part in Moses' day too?

Since the nation of Israel under Moses no longer exists, no one is bound by the civil laws or the punishments assigned for breaking them as found in the Old Testament. It is not the Christian's mission to adopt those laws in place of our own either. The New Testament suggests nothing of the sort, and so the rule stands: if not repeated in the New, it's only for the Old.

Anyone who pits these civil laws against marriage today shows that they have no firm knowledge of the Scriptures. If others suggest that these laws, along with other parts of the Old Testament, were too cruel, and they hold that out as a reason to ignore the Bible in regard to marriage or other doctrines, they too show themselves to have a poor understanding of God's Word.

OT Laws Are Moral

The last laws in the Old Testament, which alone are relevant to our day, are those understood as the moral law. The Ten Commandments are often thought of as a good summary of God's moral law (Exodus 20:1–17). These are the laws that reflect what has been called the Golden Rule: "In everything, do to others what you would have them do to you, for this sums up the Law and the Prophets" (Matthew 7:12).

These moral laws are the laws that deal with a person's relationship with God and with his neighbor, the breaking of which is called sin. Those who live a life in which they choose to commit sin and refuse to abandon it in Christ will never enter into the kingdom of heaven (1 Corinthians 6:9–10).

Scripture gives the reason why it is not possible to enter into the kingdom of God while living a lifestyle of willful sin. "It is impossible for those who have once been enlightened, who have tasted the heavenly gift, who have shared in the Holy Spirit, who have tasted the goodness of the Word of God and the powers of the coming age and who have fallen away, to be brought back to repentance. To their loss, *they are crucifying the Son of God all over again and subjecting him to public disgrace"* (Hebrews 6:4–6, emphasis added).

A summary of the moral law and the extent to which it is to be followed is found in the parable of the Good Samaritan (Luke 10:25–37). We have already spent a great deal of time on the subject of moral law in previous sections as we addressed homosexuality and sexual immorality in general. These are the laws that are revealed in the Old Testament and are repeated in the New. Therefore, they do not fall into the other categories of laws that no longer apply.

In the New Testament, the Christian's response to God's grace revolves around keeping oneself morally pure in relation to others and God (Romans 12:1–2). Again, this life of purity is offered up by a follower of Jesus out of love for Jesus, who saved us from the curse that resulted from breaking the law (Galatians 3:13). It is not out of a sense of obligation or fear that these commands are to be kept. The motivation is one only of the gospel of Christ.

Just read the last sections of many of the letters of Paul in the New Testament, and you will see that his words are full of encouragement to live a life of thanks, purity, morality, and faithfulness to God for the love the Lord gave us on the cross.

Perhaps Paul summed it up best when he touched on the moral law and the appropriate view of it in light of Christ. "Shall we go on sinning so that grace may increase? By no means! We are those who have died to sin; how can we live in it any longer? Or don't you know that all of us who were baptized into Christ Jesus were baptized into his death? We were therefore buried with him through baptism into death in order that, just as Christ was raised from the dead through the glory of the Father, we too may live a new life" (Romans 6:1–3).

The Unlawful Practice of Polygamy

When addressing the topic of homosexuality, there will be some who struggle to understand why homosexuality is condemned as a sin while another immoral practice in the Old Testament seemed to be condoned. The temptation in this perception is again to ignore what the Bible says in various places and to adopt a belief system of one's own choosing. A consideration of the immoral practice of polygamy in the Old Testament at this time would prove helpful. Again, it is good for us to be ready to give an answer to anyone who asks for the hope we have.

It would be unfair to say that Abraham, the father of the faith (Genesis 12:1–3) was a polygamist. He did have relations with Hagar, a maidservant to his wife, and this was at the request of his wife, Sarah. Her hope was to provide her husband with a son. Whatever the case, if not technically polygamy, this was adultery.

Since this was displeasing to God, Abraham and Sarah very quickly found out that this was contrary to God's design in the suffering that followed. Abraham did not remain with Hagar. There was jealousy and infighting in the family. The manmade arrangement to provide a son had become a cruel hardship for all of them (Genesis 21:8–10). I consider it just another proof that God gives his laws for a reason. Polygamy and adultery are forbidden, and when they are embraced, they naturally provide devastating consequences. It's the same with all sin.

Jacob, also called Israel, would be referred to as a polygamist. However, knowing the struggles he endured in his life, my guess is that he would have advised no one else to follow in his footsteps in that regard. Moreover, his fall into polygamy was arguably unintentional. His marrying of more than one woman was brought about by his father-in-law's initial deception on Jacob's wedding night.

At the last minute, Laban swapped his daughters, which ultimately led to Jacob's taking them both in marriage. Because of that sibling rivalry, his wives would go on to encourage him to have relations with two of their maidservants for the purpose of having more children so that one wife could outdo the other. Still, one must own up to one's own personal choices. And did Jacob ever pay dearly for the choices he made!

Jacob's sin of polygamy provided the worst kind of sibling rivalry a father could ever imagine. He would suffer seeing his sons commit immorality, even within the family. He would come to find infighting, jealousy, murderous scheming, and years of his sons covering up an unspeakable deed—selling Jacob's favorite son, Joseph, into slavery. Just read the second half of Genesis, and you'll see what polygamy offers to a family. It would be unfair to say that God was okay with that. There's no mention of such a thing anywhere.

Go on to read about the kings and any other occurrences you find of polygamy. You will not find the Lord condoning such a practice. Solomon, for example, who had more wives than perhaps anybody else, as well as concubines, is believed by some to have lost his faith in God for what may have been much of his life. In fact, there is a warning in the Old Testament about taking many wives, because many wives will lead a heart astray into idolatry (Deuteronomy 17:17).

If Solomon was the writer of Ecclesiastes, as the opening of the book seems to suggest, it is clear that the life he lived apart from God in polygamy and excess was admittedly a waste. It was a life he confessed to be entirely futile and empty. That's always how it is in a life full of sin. That's much of the message of Ecclesiastes.

There is a principle we should also keep in mind when it comes to polygamy: description is not prescription. This rule means that just because you see it in the Bible, this doesn't mean that God's okay with it or that you should do it. Noah got drunk after the flood (Genesis 9:21). Moses killed a man (Exodus 2:12). David committed adultery with a woman, and he had her husband murdered (2 Samuel 11:4, 15). Besides that, he too had many wives. The people in Josiah's day chose not to bother reading the Bible or to take it very seriously. It got so bad that they actually lost the Word of God (2 Kings 22:8). God was not pleased with any of this, though in some cases, God did not address these things outright but allowed them to happen.

We'd be mistaken to think that if anyone made it into the Bible as a hero, it would be because he was some kind of saint. Quite the opposite was true. If any individuals made it into the Bible and are now respected, it's not because they were perfect on their own. It's because God redeemed them and covered over a multitude of sins through Jesus' blood. It means that they trusted in Christ their Savior and ultimately had repentant hearts.

Polygamy falls under description, not prescription. Polygamy also falls under condemnation in the New Testament. When Jesus defined marriage in Matthew 19 and referred to Genesis 2 to do that, it became clear that marriage is only for one man and one woman. It always was meant to be that way in both the Old and New Testament times. Marriage was never permitted to include more than two people or two of the same kind. Paul affirmed this truth when he called for a Christian leader to be "the husband of but one wife" (1 Timothy 3:2; Titus 1:6). We should assume that what God demands of the leaders he also looks for in his people.

There's one last thought that we should remember when it comes to any waywardness in Old Testament times in comparison to the last days of human history in the New Testament age. All things that were to be revealed have been revealed now. The only thing left is the end. The time for ignorance over sin and our salvation has come to an end.

Paul shared this message with the people of Athens in his day, when he told them, "The times of ignorance God overlooked but now he demands all people everywhere to repent" (Acts 17:30). There may have been times in the Old Testament when the Lord did not fully address sweeping societal sins. Polygamy may have been one of those sins. But now that time is gone.

Jesus drew our attention to this reality of the last days, for he said on the night before he was crucified, "When [the Holy Spirit] comes, he will convict the world concerning sin and righteousness and judgment" (John 16:8). The New Testament in all its fullness has accomplished this prophecy of Jesus.

Paul and Marriage

We began this lengthy section by focusing on how people are perverting the Scriptures in hopes of redefining marriage. Allow me to close our discussion on traditional marriage with the greatest reason why we Christians should look to uphold marriage as God created it.

In Ephesians 5:31–32, Paul pointed out that the institution of marriage was designed for divine purposes. This was always God's intent, but the true reason for marriage was hidden until Christ was revealed and came to his people. Notice how the apostle Paul picked up on the sacred meaning behind marriage—revealed in the last days—as he wrote, "'Therefore a man shall leave his father and mother and hold fast to his wife, and the two shall become one flesh.' This mystery is profound, and I am saying that it refers to Christ and the church" (Ephesians 5:31–32).

That passage from Ephesians ultimately explains why we Christians are to be so adamant about preserving marriage as it is. There are indeed earthly blessings to marriage, which no society can do without. Marriage is one of the pillars that any successful society is built upon. But when we understand that marriage is to be a picture of Christ and the church he purified, the institution becomes something that cannot be altered or done away with except by gross sacrilege and eternal peril to our human race.

Now it makes sense why all forms of sexual immorality are so displeasing to God, along with adultery and divorce. Those things can only give a false picture of Christ and his church. Can anyone imagine Jesus giving up on us? Can anyone imagine his holy church abandoning him? How could Jesus ever choose to be united to anything other than his bride, the church? How could the church ever choose anything but Jesus? The universe would fall apart if any of those things ever happened between Jesus and the church. It borders on blasphemy even to suggest such hypotheticals.

To redefine marriage in any way other than the way Paul rightly defined it in Ephesians 5 is to shatter the picture of Christ and the church, a picture planted deep within every culture, just waiting for the rain of the Word to bring forth the mystery. This is why marriage has always been a universal institution. This is why it's so devastating to tamper with this institution in any way. The preservation of marriage enables both man and woman to practice true love and to spread the gospel of Christ by word and example unlike any other relationship can. The destruction of the institution of marriage removes one more critical way for Christ to be proclaimed and for Christ-like love to be experienced. This is just one more thing the world doesn't need as it continues to fall apart.

Marriage can never be redefined. At least it cannot be redefined in the eyes of God, whose perspective is the only one that matters. In the process of trying to redefine it, even though we can't, we only so obscure the definition of marriage that we won't know what to make of it anymore as a society. In that sobering reality, we are in danger of losing the many blessings that God promised to give through it, which especially includes an understanding of Christ and the church.

I pray that every Christian can see all the more this truth and what's at stake in this discussion. Marriage has everything to do with the gospel of Christ (Ephesians 5:31–32).

13

Somewhere over the Rainbow

The Meaning of the Rainbow

Somewhere over the rainbow, our heavenly Father waits patiently, full of grace and mercy, not at all wishing for the sons and daughters of men to perish (Ezekiel 18:30). There's no greater proof of that truth than Jesus' sacrifice on the cross. Jesus didn't die without reason, and he didn't only die for the worst of us, as if some could be saved without him (Galatians 2:21; Psalm 49:7). Christ died so that no one should perish (John 3:16).

There is no doubt that God is a patient God, but for our own sakes, his patience will not last forever. He will not let us destroy ourselves completely. He will not let us leave a legacy of destruction for endless generations (Genesis 6–9). The essence of this truth is captured in the meaning of the rainbow.

Who hasn't seen the great vision of a rainbow crossing ominous clouds on the horizon as the sun shatters the darkness? How many of us have ever stopped to consider what a rainbow really is and if there's really any meaning behind it? Rainbows are truly an amazing phenomenon of nature.

When you stand looking at one after a storm has passed, doesn't it just bring a smile to your face? Aren't you compelled to go and find someone else to share that vision with you? When does a rainbow in the sky *not* bring sighs of amazement from young and old alike? I don't believe this is by accident. In fact, I know it isn't. Surely God has set eternity in the hearts of us all (Ecclesiastes 3:11) and has purposed the rainbow to teach us that he is indeed looking over all that we do with keen interest (Genesis 9:8–17).

The Rainbow and the Flood

The first time the rainbow showed up in the Holy Scriptures was in the days just after the worldwide flood (Genesis 6:1–9:17). If you recall, God sent those floodwaters as judgment against a world hardened by unbelief and wickedness. People had been tampering with marriage, among other things (Genesis 6:2), and in God's eyes the fabric of society was unraveling. It got to a point where everyone only celebrated what was evil.

Their celebrities, whom they exalted above all others, were those whom God deemed the very bottom of the barrel. The heroes they lifted up were so depraved that God declared them to be "the fallen ones" (or *Nephilim*, Genesis 6:4). No one could leave anything but a legacy of destruction for any of the generations yet to come (Genesis 6:5). All but one family had entirely rejected the gospel. The Scriptures say that the Lord wept over the fact that he had even made us at all (Genesis 6:6).

Among all the people on the face of the earth, there was only one who was still looking for the Messiah to come. This man and his family alone had a relationship with God (Genesis 3:15; Genesis 6:9; Hebrews 11:7). That man was Noah. God told Noah and his family to build a ship large enough to fit all the different kinds of animals in it, because the whole world was going to flood.

The people of Noah's day would have 120 years to repent in order to turn back the tide of those floodwaters, or at least to be delivered by them (Genesis 6:3). Sadly, no one heeded the Lord's call to return

Rainbow Savior

to him. No one listened to the thunderous warning in every hammer blow that built the great ark. No one listened to the faithful preaching of Noah as he cried out that God's time of grace was nearly depleted. The people of that world laughed at him and thought he had lost his mind (1 Peter 3:19–20; 2 Peter 2:5; 3:9–10).

Finally the floodwaters came, and it was all over. While everyone continued on with everyday life—marrying and giving into marriage, eating and drinking, buying and selling—life came to an abrupt end (Luke 17:26–37). Everyone perished except Noah, the seven with him, and the animals the Lord provided.

After the survivors had spent about a year in the ark, the waters finally subsided. God was going to give the human race one last time of grace. With all his heart, he wanted the descendants of Noah—you and me—to live in the light of that grace and never perish.

The whole thing was a miraculous event, but God is known for the impossible, isn't he? Not only can he create everything out of nothing and rescue some by water, but he can save the whole world by a cross. He can even soften the hardest of hearts to believe. Therefore, he can still give us all the hope we need and the power to turn it all around if we only listen to what he is saying.

This is where the rainbow comes into play. The rainbow points to the hope of God's grace to change us all before it's too late.

> "I will never again curse the ground because of man, for the intention of man's heart is evil from his youth. Neither will I ever again strike down every living creature as I have done. While the earth remains, seedtime and harvest, cold and heat, summer and winter, day and night, shall not cease … I have set my bow in the cloud, and it shall be a sign of the covenant between me and the earth. When I bring clouds over the earth and the bow is seen in the clouds, I will remember my covenant that is between me and you and every living creature of all flesh. And the waters shall never again become a flood to destroy all

flesh. When the bow is in the clouds, I will see it and remember the everlasting covenant between God and every living creature of all flesh that is on the earth." God said to Noah, "This is the sign of the covenant that I have established between me and all flesh that is on the earth." (Genesis 8:21–22; 9:13–16)

The word for "bow" (rainbow) in the Hebrew language as translated here is the same as a war bow (Psalm 44:6). This would seem to indicate that the rainbow is God's war bow, which he hangs up in the sky to no longer wage war against sinners for their sin, at least for a time, so that they might repent and be saved. As long as the war bow hangs in the sky, there is a time of grace for sinners to turn from their sins, lest they face the wrath of his bow.

Some have also noted that the bow is pointed toward heaven where God himself dwells. Was he implying by the direction of the bow that he himself would pay the price for sin one day and endure divine judgment on our behalf on the cross? The Scriptures do declare Jesus to be both God's polished arrow in his quiver (Isaiah 49:2) and, if you will, the bull's-eye for God's wrath over sin (Isaiah 53:5,10; 2 Corinthians 5:21). Whatever the case, Jesus Christ is undeniably the reason for God's ongoing patience and grace.

The promise of the rainbow is that God will show himself to be a gracious and longsuffering God in the face of ever increasing wickedness. God has already proven himself faithful in this promise in giving his Son, Jesus, at the cross. There is no other place where you'll find the infinite patience of God displayed in the face of the absolute evil of humanity. That means that Jesus is at the center of the rainbow promise, and he alone is the reason it still appears in the sky to this day (Revelation 4:3; Revelation 5:6). For that reason, he can rightfully be called the Rainbow Savior.

God will remain patient until all hope is gone for the human race, until, one by one, all the people of the world harden their hearts and refuse the gospel of Jesus Christ. Only then will everything dissolve in one last supernatural event known as Judgment Day (2 Peter 3:5–7). At the end of time, only those who are like Noah—placing faith in the Messiah as they turn from their sin—will be saved. Friends, the rainbow is a sign that our time of grace to turn to the Lord is running out. That is the meaning of the rainbow.

The Rainbow and Judah

The Scriptures declare the meaning of the bow a couple more crucial times as the Word of God moves along, and the meaning is given further detail with increasing intensity. While God's people were in the darkest hours of their Babylonian captivity because of their sin, when all seemed to be lost in judgment as in the days of the flood, the rainbow showed up again as a ray of hope.

In Ezekiel's ministry (593–571 BC), we find a parallel to the time of the pre-flood world. Judah's days had become just like Noah's. Very few were left holding on to the promise of the Messiah and the salvation he would bring. Unlike in Noah's day, however, the rainbow took on a more definite and miraculous form of grace.

In the first chapter of Ezekiel's prophecy, he shared his opening vision with the faithful: "Like the appearance of the bow that is in the cloud on the day of rain, so was the appearance of the brightness all around. Such was the appearance of the likeness of the glory of the LORD. [The glory of the Lord is God's presence of grace.] And when I saw it, I fell on my face" (Ezekiel 1:28).

The God who made the first promise about the rainbow of grace was now himself enveloped by the rainbow, and for one purpose: He intended to deliver his grace personally to a world in desperate need of it. In Ezekiel's vision, therefore, God was pictured as the Rainbow Savior.

The rest of Ezekiel's book goes on to point out that the rainbow-encircled presence of the Lord was fading off into the distance because of Judah's sin (Ezekiel 8–11). This signified that the times would get a little worse for Judah before they'd get better. God seemed to be leaving them in judgment.

Ezekiel used this vision to teach the people that there was a limit to the time of God's grace. One day it would forever disappear. So the prophet taught them that if they would repent, the Lord would relent. Like Noah, Ezekiel preached that God does not want anybody to perish (Ezekiel 18). This is the message of all the true prophets of every age (Luke 24:44–47). This, again, is the message of the rainbow.

By grace, at the end of Ezekiel's prophecy, the Lord came back in his rainbow-encircled glory. This would be a sign to Ezekiel and the people of Judah that God's grace had not yet run out for those in the fallen world. God was declaring that he would bring the people of Judah out of captivity one last time to fulfill the greater promise of salvation. Then he himself would come with salvation, marking the beginning of the end.

Toward the conclusion of Ezekiel's work, we read about the Lord's coming in accordance with the rainbow promise: "Then he led me to the gate, the gate facing east. And behold, the glory of the God of Israel was coming from the east. And the sound of his coming was like the sound of many waters, and the earth shone with his glory" (Ezekiel 43:1–2).

That section from Ezekiel 43:1–2 is a prophecy of the Messiah. Ezekiel saw that the very Christ, the glory of the Lord, would come to his people to save them. He would enter from the east from over the Mount of Olives, which was just what Jesus did on the Sunday known as Palm Sunday when he was proclaimed king over all (Matthew 21:1–11). At the close of that Palm Sunday procession, Jesus entered through the golden gate of the temple grounds, the eastern gate. He had come to grace his temple with his presence, just as Ezekiel foresaw.

By week's end, Jesus would fulfill his role as the first, last, and only Savior of all people. He would tear in two the veil of the temple that divided sinners from God. Jesus alone would open the way for sinners to cross somewhere over the rainbow into the presence of God, the Father, and live.

This was all that God ever wanted. On the third day after his crucifixion, Jesus proved that such a hope was reality when he triumphed over the grave. Beloved of the Lord, this is all a historical fact, as Jesus' tomb remains empty to this day (1 Corinthians 15).

The Rainbow and the End

The last place we read about the rainbow is in the book of Revelation. It is in this last record of Holy Scripture that Ezekiel's vision returns and comes into full view. At the conclusion of the Bible, we finally see who is at the center of the rainbow-encircled glory of the Lord, and his identity is unmistakable. The apostle John shared the vision with us.

> He who sat there [on the throne of God] had the appearance of jasper and carnelian, and around the throne was a rainbow that had the appearance of an emerald ... Between the throne and the four living creatures and among the elders I saw a Lamb standing, as though it had been slain, with seven horns [all-powerful] and with seven eyes [all-knowing], which are the seven spirits of God [the Holy Spirit] sent out into all the earth [everywhere present]. And he went and took the scroll [the future] from the right hand of him who was seated on the throne [God Almighty] ... And the Lamb [was] in the midst of the throne. (Revelation 4:3; 5:6; 7:17)

John bore witness to the Rainbow Savior, and it was Jesus.

Jesus is literally at the heart of the rainbow throne, and as such, he has all authority to reign over the rest of human history. This is the will of the Father. On behalf of the rainbow promise, then, Jesus sends his Spirit throughout the earth to proclaim a final saving message through all his messengers (Revelation 10). It's the exact message that God proclaimed after the flood, only with all the details filled in. This is the gospel at the culmination of the ages. Humankind's future in this broken world will now last only as long as it takes to spread the news to all nations that there is a Savior from sin: Jesus Christ.

In spite of this universal proclamation, all hearts will eventually turn away, leaving only a remnant of people as in Noah's and Ezekiel's day (Matthew 24:22). Once the mission is accomplished to rescue all of God's own, God will take up his war bow and destroy sin and all who embrace it, once and for all. At that time, all creation will be restored, and God's people will be saved.

Who of us knows the true meaning of the rainbow nowadays? How many people, when they see a rainbow, think, "There's God's grace again! Thank you, Father, for hanging your war bow up just a little while longer! Thanks for not giving up on us just yet! There's still a little time left to turn away from all sin and take shelter in the ark of Christ, the ark God built with the wood of an old rugged cross!"

The true meaning of the rainbow is foreign to so many people today and, sadly, to many churches. Although rainbow banners are being lifted up more and more, the message of its real meaning is all but forgotten. Is it finally time for the rainbow-encircled glory of the Lord to fade off into the horizon, never to be seen again? Could it possibly return through the faithful preaching of the Word of God, or are we finally at the end? God alone knows.

But I know he still doesn't want anyone to perish. I know that God wants all to come to know him and to be saved through Jesus Christ (1 Timothy 2:3–6). I know this through the Word of God. I am even reminded of this whenever the rainbow appears to break the threat of a storm.

The Rainbow and Our Children

Because of the true meaning of the rainbow, I'm glad to see it so often among children and toddlers. Rainbows fill their books, cover their toys and clothes, and decorate their day-care centers and schools. All these places where the rainbow appears can provide opportunities to share with little ones the love of God in Christ, and especially his forgiveness in the face of wrongdoing. Could there be anything greater than to tell children, when they've done wrong and feel bad, "You're forgiven! Jesus loves you! Remember the promise of the rainbow? That rainbow proves that he loves us all, even if we fall into sin!"?

We can then go on to show them the proper response to forgiveness: to go and "sin no more." At the very least, faith in Christ means that we strive to turn from sin. This is a message for all of God's children especially any of our youth who have lost their way and become steeped in an immoral lifestyle.

I like that rainbows fill the lives of little children, along with unicorns[70] and whatever other fairytale creatures are attached to rainbows. Perhaps those magical creatures can provide more opportunities to talk about the love of God and the things he has planned for us above, things that are beyond our comprehension (1 John 3:1–2; Ephesians 3:20). We could use all those things to make believe and imagine what heaven will actually be like when we get there. Are those fairy-tale creatures no longer fairy tales there? What

---

[70] Though the symbol of the unicorn, like the symbol of the rainbow, is being connected to more perverse meanings today, centuries after the apostles and up to the days of the Reformation, the unicorn became a symbol of Christ within the visible church. Some of the details of the symbolism of the unicorn are as follows. The nature of the unicorn is miraculous, which is symbolic of the nature of the Christ incarnate. In the Scriptures, the "horn" denotes power, symbolizing Christ's omnipotence and oneness with God the Father and the Spirit. The horn also symbolizes purity, as does the white color of the unicorn. The idea was also promoted that only a virgin maiden could call for a unicorn and contain it. This symbolizes the virgin birth of Christ and the fact that the Christ willingly came to us by way of Mary's womb. Another idea promoted in connection with a virgin was that the unicorn could only be hunted and killed if it willingly rested its head on a virgin's lap. This last idea was used to symbolize the truth about Christ's sacrifice. He was born of a virgin that he might willingly give up his life for those who would look to slay him.

will it be like to see heaven—and Jesus at the center of the rainbow throne?

You and I, as adults, might not be inclined to use our imaginations much in this way because of our age—or perhaps because of the hard world we live in. We might think it's awkward and uncomfortable to talk like that to children. But if you ever talk to children about the unbelievable things God has in store for those who love him, you'll see that it's not child's play at all. I think we'll find the opposite to be true.

We will be amazed when we hear from the mouths of children all the possibilities above. We'll especially note too, as they talk, that these are things they don't have any difficulty believing in. If the Lord says it, it's enough for them! We can learn something from our children about faith (Luke 18:17). What joy can come to the heart of a child—and all of us—when we imagine out loud about the reality that waits for us somewhere over the rainbow!

Do you know what saddens me, though, about the images of the rainbow and the fairy-tale creatures that accompany them these days? It's the newer messages being attached to them by the world. How will our children, as they grow old, escape those newer meanings that will only hurt them and their relationship with Christ if they embrace them?

The only way to help our young people is to teach them the real meaning of the rainbow and to teach them all the Scriptures that go with it. This is the only way faith will survive in our day. It's the only way it has ever survived (Romans 10:17). Of course, we can only teach the next generation if we remain students of God's Word ourselves. In a sense, we can save our youth and ourselves in Christ, if we keep a close watch on what we do and on our teaching, and if we never give up on those things (1 Timothy 4:16).

We can teach our children from the Scriptures how to befriend everyone, while remaining unmoved in their convictions. We can teach them of Daniel, who was not afraid to face the lion's den, or Shadrach, Meshach, and Abednego, who were unafraid to face the fiery furnace (Daniel 6; Daniel 3). Their bravery flowed from a thorough knowledge of God, his love for them, and God's love for a hardened people. These are all historical accounts that have been taught to children in generations past. Are we teaching them now?

For the sake of our children, we must not go the way of Eli, whose sons were destroyed because of their sin and because of Eli's failure to practice tough love with them as a parent (1 Samuel 2:27–36). The Scriptures are clear: if you want to be a willing party to the death of your children, don't raise them in the Lord and don't discipline them either (Proverbs 22:3–6; Proverbs 19:18). Instead we must teach our kids that the beginning of wisdom is to love and respect the Lord and all he says (Proverbs 1:7).

Young people need to understand the real spiritual forces involved in this discussion on homosexuality. The world is at war with Christianity, and most of the world might not even know it. Many Christians may have forgotten this fact too. Make no mistake; there is a real war going on for all our souls, which is just as the Lord taught us (Genesis 3:1–15; Revelation 12–13).

We can arm our children for the battle they cannot avoid. Their sole weapon must be the Word of love for the sinner and hatred for the sin that threatens us all. We are not at war with flesh and blood but with all that's wrong and entangles us in the world. We are all on the same side as the human race. Either we are free, or we are imprisoned behind enemy lines. Our enemies are all the ungodly influences we find everywhere, inside of us and outside in the world (Matthew 15:19; Romans 12:2).

The apostle Paul's words teach us about this spiritual warfare, a war that always needs to remain on the forefront of our minds and on the minds of our children.

> Finally, be strong in the Lord and in the strength of his might. Put on the whole armor of God, that you may be able to stand against the schemes of the devil. For we do not wrestle against flesh and blood, but against the

rulers, against the authorities, against the cosmic powers over this present darkness, against the spiritual forces of evil in the heavenly places. Therefore take up the whole armor of God, that you may be able to withstand in the evil day, and having done all, to stand firm. Stand therefore, having fastened on the belt of truth, and having put on the breastplate of righteousness, and, as shoes for your feet, having put on the readiness given by the gospel of peace. In all circumstances take up the shield of faith, with which you can extinguish all the flaming darts of the evil one; and take the helmet of salvation, and the sword of the Spirit, which is the word of God, praying at all times in the Spirit, with all prayer and supplication. To that end keep alert with all perseverance, making supplication for all the saints. (Ephesians 6:10–18)

Lot and His Children

Our modern situation and society's growing callousness to the truth of the real meaning of the rainbow reminds me of an account from Genesis 19. It's an account about a man and his children. In Genesis we read about Lot, who was found seated in the city gateway of Sodom. To be seated at the gateway of a city in those days was to have a place among the ruling council. The last place you can read about Lot's living arrangements before this account is in Genesis 13:10–12. At that time, he was only living in the plains of Sodom and Gomorrah. How does a righteous man move from the country into the heart of a wicked city?

I'm not saying that Lot had lost the Lord. The apostle Peter reminds us that Lot was a righteous man who was distressed by the unlawful people of the town of Sodom. The Scripture says he was highly distressed by what he heard and saw (2 Peter 2:6–8). Perhaps

Rainbow Savior

in his move to the city he was hoping to be a better influence on the people there. We don't know.

At the same time, I wonder if the Lord was seeking to rescue Lot, who perhaps moved for foolish reasons. Maybe Lot was beginning to lose his faith in the face of increasing wickedness.

Whatever Lot's condition, we can at least be aware of the "frog in the pot" syndrome. When immorality slowly heats up and goes unchecked, we shouldn't be surprised to find many who are overcome by the heat of falsehood. We should not be surprised if we suddenly find ourselves living in the gateway of a wicked town either. Here's part of the account of Lot and his children.

> Two angels came to Sodom in the evening, and Lot was sitting in the gate of Sodom. When Lot saw them, he rose to meet them and bowed himself with his face to the earth and said, "My lords, please turn aside to your servant's house and spend the night and wash your feet. Then you may rise up early and go on your way."
>
> They said, "No; we will spend the night in the town square." But he pressed them strongly; so they turned aside to him and entered his house. And he made them a feast and baked unleavened bread, and they ate. But before they lay down, the men of the city, the men of Sodom, both young and old, all the people to the last man, surrounded the house.
>
> And they called to Lot, "Where are the men who came to you tonight? Bring them out to us, that we may know them" [a euphemism for "to have sexual intercourse with them"].[71] Lot went out to the men at the entrance, shut the

---

[71] Some argue that the sin of Sodom wasn't homosexuality but was instead inhospitality. Jude verse 7, however, says that the sin of Sodom and Gomorrah was sexual immorality and perversion. Nowhere does Jude mention inhospitality, although the actions of the Sodomites were truly inhospitable in the most extreme sense of the word. In the end, what led Sodom and Gomorrah to judgment was

door after him, and said, "I beg you, my brothers, do not act so wickedly. Behold, I have two daughters who have not known any man. Let me bring them out to you, and do to them as you please. Only do nothing to these men, for they have come under the shelter of my roof."

But they said, "Stand back!" And they said, "This fellow came to sojourn, and he has become the judge! Now we will deal worse with you than with them." Then they pressed hard against the man Lot, and drew near to break the door down. But the men reached out their hands and brought Lot into the house with them and shut the door. And they struck with blindness the men who were at the entrance of the house, both small and great, so that they wore themselves out groping for the door.

Then the men said to Lot, "Have you anyone else here? Sons-in-law, sons, daughters, or anyone you have in the city, bring them out of the place. For we are about to destroy this place, because the outcry against its people has become great before the LORD, and the LORD has sent us to destroy it." So Lot went out and said to his sons-in-law, who were to marry his daughters, "Up! Get out of this place, for the LORD is about to destroy the city." But he seemed to his sons-in-law to be jesting. (Genesis 19:1–14)

In this text, the saddest thing for Lot is what we find at the very end. His sons-in-law didn't take him seriously when he told them about the critical situation they all were in. As a result, they didn't escape the city. They perished in fiery judgment with the rest.

I wonder about Lot and the choices he made as a parent. Did he share his faith with his daughters at all when they were growing up? I would assume he did in some way (2 Corinthians 4:13). Did Lot's children ever take him seriously when he warned them about those

---

their total disregard for God's Word, disregard that inevitably showed itself in sin, including both homosexuality and inhospitality, among other sins.

two cities? They may have. They also may have become influenced by the world because of where Lot chose to live. I guess it may matter where one chooses to call home, whether it's a place where you can hear God's Word in all truth and purity, or one where you can't.

In the end, it's evident that Lot's daughters struggled to live their faith, if they had any faith at all. It seems they were unwise to be engaged to men of those cities who wouldn't listen to the Lord's warning. It appears that they were not effective as witnesses of God's truth to their future husbands, if they witnessed at all. This may be pure speculation, although I don't believe it's without merit. What Lot's daughters did with their father after those cities were destroyed was simply ungodly (Genesis 19:31–32). Whatever may have been the case, Lot left a tough lesson that we and our children are to learn from.

The Double Rainbow

Having heard the voice of our Rainbow Savior, we now move on with him in our hearts, ready to give an answer to anyone who asks for the hope we have (1 Peter 3:15). We are ready to declare the praises of him who called us out of our darkness into his wonderful light (1 Peter 2:9). In the hopes of declaring his praises wisely, I humbly offer two ways to begin proclaiming the Savior's praise in regard to this topic.

Share the message of this work *with fellow Christians*. Share the message of this book with another Christian who especially struggles with or is entangled in homosexuality. Offer to go over the message of this book together. You don't have to proceed in the order the chapters appear. You can pick and choose the sections that fit most appropriately. Feel free to pull out excerpts, as if those words were from your own heart, which is often a much better approach. And these words are indeed your words, because they are from the Scriptures, which are the heritage of every Christian.

Ask other Christians among your family and friends to join you in this study too. Perhaps your Christian loved ones could go on to encourage their particular congregations and leaders to hold a Bible study or a small group discussion on this topic, guided by the Rainbow Savior. You can find more resources at *www.rainbowsavior.com*.

As you, dear Christians, discuss these things, don't argue with anybody. Just listen to your fellow Christians, especially those struggling with any concepts, and lovingly point them back to whatever part of the work is most applicable. The Lord also promises to give you the words to speak at just the right time so that you can say what needs to be said (Matthew 10:18–20). Be encouraged!

As for speaking to the *world*, I would encourage a more general message of Christ and a different approach that does not focus specifically on the issue of homosexuality where possible. As was discussed earlier, homosexuality is not the issue. Our hope in Christ to deliver us from all sin is the issue. This is always the issue and the only issue with the nonbeliever. Once faith is won over in the heart, all the issues will fall into place by God's grace. I would, therefore, encourage you to only speak to the world of the general need for repentance as the apostle Paul did in Athens (Acts 17:22–31).

In our call to the world for general repentance over all sin, I would also advise that you speak in the first person plural (we, us). Let's invite everyone to join with us in turning away from all that is sinful and toward the Lord Jesus Christ to be saved. Be bold to add to this truth that one day Jesus will come again to judge all people and that only those who repent, are baptized, and believe on the Lord Jesus Christ will be saved (Acts 2:38). Tell everyone that we Christians proclaim all of this in the simple hope that everyone might share with us in the resurrection of the dead unto life eternal (Acts 23:6).

To provide a way to speak to the world of the need for general repentance—and to utilize the issue of homosexuality as a springboard to do just that—let me suggest that you use the symbol of the rainbow, with some modifications, of course. Among Christian people, let the symbol of the rainbow return to its original meaning of calling the world to repent before the end of all things comes. I would suggest that a restoration of the rainbow and its original meaning as a symbol for the church is possible and worth the effort. After all, the rainbow belongs to the Christian. It is a symbol that God ordained for the calling of all people back to himself. It is found in the Holy Scriptures! In fact, it is still found in the sky. Should we Christians give up on that symbol and its meaning, or should we resurrect it? It seems like the latter is more in keeping with what Christians are all about!

In order to be successful in our efforts to utilize the rainbow as a witness to Christ, a couple of modifications will have to be made to the symbol. Otherwise, there will only be confusion among the world and fellow Christians about its meaning. As I see it, there need to be two changes, with the second being of the utmost importance.

The first change to the rainbow symbol for a Christian to use would be to reverse the rainbow colors so that they appear like the illustration on the front cover of this work. We can create some rich symbolism with this reversal of colors. Let me explain.

Have you ever seen a double rainbow? They do appear from time to time. If seeing a rainbow is rare, seeing a double rainbow is much more so. These double rainbows appear when the sun breaks through a lot of rain on a dark enough sky and for a long enough time. When that happens, another rainbow shows up somewhere high above the first. This is the war bow, where all the colors run in reverse, the opposite of the rainbow below it. I think of it as the greater rainbow, although it is harder to see.

I see a parallel between the phenomenon of the double rainbow and the two meanings of the rainbow we have today. The greater, higher biblical message of what the rainbow means is as rare as the appearance of the second rainbow in nature that hangs high above the first. And just as the colors are the same but run in reverse, so the two messages are similar (grace) but couldn't be more opposite.

The more common meaning of the rainbow today makes grace into a license to sin. The higher message reverses that thinking. The original meaning now attached to the greater rainbow by this work is meant to communicate that grace is running out. The rainbow in reverse proclaims that the time to repent is the present time, before judgment comes. Today is the day of salvation (Isaiah 55:6)! This is the new meaning of the rainbow, which is simply a return to the first meaning ever attached to it.

The second and most important—and essential—modification to the symbol is to put Christ crucified at the center of the rainbow, as the front cover of this work does (Revelation 4:3; 5:6; 7:17). What better way to modify the rainbow than to have Christ on the cross at the center of it to show us all why God's grace has not yet run out for this world? It's entirely biblical.

Christ died that all might be saved, and God has not yet ended this world, for one reason and one reason alone: he is being patient with everybody and wants all to come to repentance before the end (2 Peter 3:9). In further shaping the cross into the form of an arrow, we can also remind everyone that the rainbow is God's war bow and that Christ, who died for all, is coming again, but at that time, Jesus will become the arrow of God's wrath and judgment for all who reject him (Isaiah 49:2–7).

Use the new rainbow, especially if you feel compelled to do something about this issue of homosexuality, which is so troubling to the Christian. Let people ask you about the rainbow in reverse and about Christ who is at the center of it. I hope that people inquire about its meaning. In our answers, though, let them know that the true meaning of the rainbow is the biblical one, which calls for universal repentance over all sin.

And be sure to avoid the topic of homosexuality with nonbelievers. It's not the issue, nor is this what our restored symbol is all about. Instead, strive to help nonbelievers understand what Christ did for all of us as signified by the original rainbow. After you tell them both law and gospel, ask them to confess what they believe about Jesus. If they reject Christ, then tell them that it really doesn't matter what you think about homosexuality. Let them know that the only thing that really matters is faith in Christ.

Following that conversation, which should end there, continue to show them love, and keep reaching out to them with the call of repentance, both law and gospel. If they confess faith in Christ, then lead them through the message of this book with all gentleness and respect—if they have lingering questions on the issue of homosexuality. Whatever you do about the subject at hand, proclaim Christ in the face of all sin! Call the world to join with you in repentance and rid the visible church of all sin and falsehood. That's the goal.

May God bless the efforts of our witness. May more and more people come to know what Christ has done for them as we point precious souls back to the gospel message of the great Rainbow Savior, Christ our Lord. To God alone be the glory!

Appendix 1

Barefoot in the Wilderness

The following is an interview with Mr. Scott Barefoot, who is familiar with the struggle between following Christ and embracing the homosexual lifestyle. Through this interview, he shares with us his past experience of being a straying sheep and his subsequent journey back to the fold of God and the Good Shepherd of our souls.

Interviewer: Scott, thank you for being willing to share with me a little about your struggles in faith and God's grace to you throughout it all. Can you share with us some things that happened to you in your life, things that tempted you to stray from your walk with the Lord into a homosexual lifestyle?

Scott Barefoot: I spent my teenage years growing up in rural Virginia back in the 1980s. During my adolescent years, I first noticed that I was different from my other friends. At a certain point, most of my buddies that I had always been friends with started noticing girls and dating. That day never arrived for me. It was not as if I ever made a conscious decision not to be interested in girls or dating. I was just content in being friends with the same guys with whom I had always been friends. I was friends with lots of girls my age, but I never saw or noticed anything beyond just friendship, i.e., there was no physical attraction. It was probably later on in high school where I was not only not attracted physically to girls but instead began developing that sort of attraction for other guys.

Also, around the age of sixteen, I began a period in my life where, for other reasons, I started becoming an apathetic Christian. I began doing a lot of volunteer work for my hometown rescue squad and started missing church fairly regularly. I also was not spending quality time in God's Word. My prayer life was faltering too. It was at this time that I went off to college, and at the university I attended, I began meeting guys who openly identified themselves as gay. So, by the time I graduated high school and went off to a public university, you could definitely see that there was a "perfect storm" brewing.

What intrigued me about many of the guys I met at the university was that they were a lot like me! They didn't fit the age-old stereotypes of gay men being extremely effeminate in actions or looks. I was even more shocked when some of these same guys said they were Christian. They even proceeded to take me through some Scripture passages that I had learned while growing up in the church, verses that I had been taught showed that homosexual activity was condemned by God. Several of them proceeded to offer a very different explanation and other interpretations that allowed for homosexuality. Unfortunately, at that time in my life, I was far too eager to buy into their ideas, and I ultimately ended up embracing the gay lifestyle.

Interviewer: Did you have any fears in your heart as you began to feel you were becoming more distant from the Lord?

Scott Barefoot: At the time I was embracing the gay lifestyle, I was still attending church—a very liberal, nondenominational church, where the pastor and a clear majority of the congregation members were also gay. During that period, I was being told that God really had no problem with my chosen lifestyle. In fact, I was told that it was my church that I had grown up in that was in error regarding God's Word.

However, in those days, if I was completely honest with myself, I'm not sure I ever was completely "at peace." I'm not sure I was ever 100 percent certain that the lifestyle I was embracing was pleasing to God. In hindsight, I can see the truth of the Scripture where we are told that God's laws are written on our hearts.

Interviewer: Can you describe any times in your life when you fully embraced your lifestyle, times when you were, humanly speaking, beyond the reach of your Lord's calling to you?

Scott Barefoot: During the majority of the time I was embracing a homosexual lifestyle, I did, in hindsight, feel a constant "void" in my life. Looking back now, I can see that the void was a result of basically thumbing my nose at God's will for my life. I continued to try to fill that void with circles of friends, same-sex relationship partners, and anyone who would tell me that what I was doing was really okay.

Interviewer: What happened that caused you to become more open to hearing the voice of your Lord again, and how long and difficult was your journey back?

Scott Barefoot: It was shortly after I was diagnosed with HIV that my world was really turned upside down. It was at this time that God, through the work of the Holy Spirit, really came into my life to help me see that the lifestyle I had been living for over a decade was not his will for my life. He began to work a change of heart in me, and he led me out of that lifestyle to repentance.

It was definitely not an immediate cause-and-effect situation. It wasn't as if I tested positive for HIV on a Friday and on Sunday found myself back in the pews of the church body I had grown up in. However, this crisis was definitely the beginning of a period where, for the first time in a long time, instead of immediately running back to my gay friends for support, I began to seek the help of some trusted Christian friends and family from my past.

In addition, I located my Bible, which had been stored away in a box, collecting dust for years. I began earnestly reading that again. I embarked on something of a fact-finding mission. I remember going to the pastor of the very liberal nondenominational church I had been attending and asking: "Pastor, obviously you and this church believe that God has no problem with those who embrace homosexuality. Can you please take me through the Scriptures and show me again how you arrive at that conclusion?" After that, I actually was able to track down the pastor of the congregation that I had grown up in—the one who had confirmed me—and I posed a similar question to him.

Ultimately, by the grace of God, I was led to leave the gay lifestyle and return to the church in the synod/denomination I grew up in. I returned to a church that proclaimed the truth and inerrancy of God's Word.

Interviewer: What struggles, if any, do you still face in your renewed walk with the Lord?

Scott Barefoot: I want to make it clear that while I was led out of the gay lifestyle to godly repentance, I did not wake up one day with a sudden physical attraction for women. In fact, struggling to resist homosexual temptations is a regular part of my life to this day. But I awake each day, invigorated and resolute in my desire to resist these continued temptations with the help of God. Is that always an easy thing to do? No. But I continue to be thankful that I have such a loving heavenly Father, a Father who led me out of embracing a life of unrepentant sin. I am thankful to my heavenly Father who sent his only Son, Jesus, to live a perfect life in my place, to die on the cross for my sins, and to rise victorious from the grave for me!

Interviewer: The Lord promises to "work out all things for our good" (Romans 8:28), and so I was wondering if you can see blessings that the Lord has brought to you or others through this great struggle of yours?

Scott Barefoot: Absolutely! Having been born into a devout Christian family and having grown up in a faithful church, I can look back and see that I often took that for granted. In fact, you could definitely say that I took it for granted to the point that I almost saw going to church on Sundays and spending time in God's Word as a chore. I definitely didn't appreciate it to the degree that I should have. As a result, one can see the connection between the period in my late teens and early twenties when I began to embrace a sinful lifestyle and the time when I became a very apathetic Christian.

Now, since being led out of that lifestyle, my devotional book and my Bible are the first things I reach for every morning. They are also one of the last things I put down before heading to bed each night. I also leave church on Sundays immediately looking forward to and counting down the days of the week until I can come back to worship God again!

Interviewer: Is there any encouragement you could share with those who struggle between faith in Christ and embracing the homosexual lifestyle?

Scott Barefoot: For the longest time, I was angry with God for creating me with what I have felt were these "in-born" homosexual tendencies. I can't begin to recount the number of times I've heard that same thing from others who are either struggling with or embracing a homosexual lifestyle.

It has also been a long road toward "getting over" those feelings and questions. But I've found comfort in the fact that, ever since the fall of Adam and Eve, we are all born with our own pet temptations toward different sin or that we develop them from early on. While

I may be a bit more open to sharing my experiences, there is not one Christian out there who is all alone in being tempted by some "pet" temptation toward sin. Many other people struggle daily with something, and homosexuality is the particular struggle I have had, a temptation that I know other Christians share.

I also find comfort in God's Word regarding the help that is available for everyone who struggles with temptation and sin. "Because [Jesus] himself suffered when tempted, he is able to help those who are being tempted" (Hebrews 2:18). "No temptation has overtaken you that is not common to man. God is faithful, and he will not let you be tempted beyond your ability" (1 Corinthians 10:13). "I can do all things through him who strengthens me" (Philippians 4:13).

Appendix 2

Barefoot in the Fold

The following is another interview with Mr. Scott Barefoot, who is familiar with the struggle between following Christ and embracing the homosexual lifestyle. Through this second interview, he shares with us his thoughts on the people of God and how they can be an encouragement to those who struggle between faith in Christ and embracing a homosexual lifestyle.

Interviewer: Scott, thanks again for being willing to share a little about your thoughts on the church and how the church can be an encouragement to any Christians who struggle with homosexuality. What do you perceive to be weaknesses of the church when it comes to the issue of homosexuality or when it comes to ministering to Christians who struggle with homosexuality?

Scott Barefoot: I would give my church and many others an A-plus regarding their understanding of the theology related to the issue of homosexuality. But I would probably give it a C-minus when it comes to the application of it in dealing with members or those who struggle with temptation toward homosexuality. In my experience, most people feel that this is something that only happens to other people, that surely no one they know would struggle with something like this.

In my opinion, this goes back to a common misconception that homosexuality or embracing a gay lifestyle is a purely conscious choice, a mere decision made by those who struggle with it. While, yes, I would agree with someone who says that embracing a gay lifestyle is a choice, homosexuality is no more or less a choice than it is for all who struggle with any other temptations of deceit, adultery, gossip, worshipping money or material things, etc.

Interviewer: What would you advise Christians to do and not to do, should they find that a fellow believer or a loved one is struggling with this issue?

Scott Barefoot: The first and most important advice I give folks is not to fall into the trap of letting their emotions and shock over the revelation take over. Don't react. Don't look at the individual who shares this as if he or she has just grown a second or third head on their shoulders. If this news comes as a complete shock, and you don't feel you are prepared to respond compassionately at the time you hear it, don't be afraid to take a step back from the situation. Don't be afraid to say, "Thank you for thinking enough of me to want to share this with me. I really do want to talk about this with you, but how about we make arrangements to meet again this time tomorrow to talk about it?"

That cooling-off period will help an individual get over the initial "shock and awe" of the situation and will diffuse his initial emotional reaction to the news. This will prevent emotion from overtaking the ability to respond and will allow for a calm, rational discussion about the situation. It also gives individuals the ability to pray about the situation, to call on trusted Christian friends for help, and to study some of God's Word regarding the issue. Make no mistake. You will need to be prepared to share God's Word with this individual.

I also remind people that they should not be under any delusion that this is going to be a quick, one-time interaction/conversation that will then be over. This could be a very long, frustrating period of time with your friend or loved one, who will most likely reject the truth of God's Word and whatever you are telling them. But don't be tempted to give up or throw in the towel! And *never* discount the power God grants through prayer, even when you seem to be hitting a brick wall in speaking to such an individual.

Interviewer: What advice would you give to pastors and elders of the church in reaching out to those who are straying or who have completely lost their way over this issue?

Scott Barefoot: Probably my first and most important advice would be to avoid treating this person any differently from the way they would speak to anyone else in a state of unrepentant sin. There is a tendency for people to rate sins that they themselves have never struggled with as somehow worse or more severe than the ones they have struggled with. In situations where people feel that way, I've found that some tend to be more heavy-handed with the Law. As I shared before, pastors or elders ought to acknowledge that the individual's initial struggles with homosexuality were nothing they consciously chose or sought out.

I feel it's also important not to reach a point of quickly "throwing in the towel." I would encourage them not to look at this as a situation where one or two interactions with someone like this will immediately result in their having a change of heart.

A couple of years ago, I was contacted by a pastor whose adult child had begun embracing a homosexual lifestyle. In one of my first interactions with this pastor, his inclination was to have his own child excommunicated from the church! I shared with him, "Pastor, can you honestly tell me that excommunication would be one of the *first* steps you would pursue in dealing with any other seemingly unrepentant sinner?" That made him stop and reconsider. I'm not at all implying that excommunication is not biblical or that it's not an eventual, loving step to take with someone embracing unrepentant sin.

Interviewer: If the church could have known anything about your situation or could have communicated to you before you strayed, what would you have wished for the church to do, if anything?

Scott Barefoot: The first thing that comes to mind is this: I don't believe my pastor or congregation ever spoke about this when I was growing up in the church. In my mind, that sort of fed into this feeling that (1) I'm the only one who struggles with something like this and (2) that this must be such a horrible sin that they don't even talk about it in church!

As I go around and speak with congregations about this subject and about my own struggles with it, I strongly encourage congregations to have open and balanced discussions about homosexuality. Again, going back to when I was growing up in the church in the 1980s, this was a subject that was virtually never discussed.

I encourage pastors to speak about it openly and in a balanced way from the pulpit. I often get asked, "Well, how early should we be talking about this with our children?" I think that the age when children are learning catechism is prime time (junior high), especially when you are discussing the sixth commandment.

I also encourage congregations to consider a topical Bible study on the subject. If someone struggling with homosexuality is part of a congregation that does this, they may think, "Hey, at least this pastor and group of Christians are willing to talk about it. Maybe it's not such an unthinkable thing to approach them about my struggles with this."